the CAN book

Text copyright © 1989 by Pascal Bussy

Published by SAF Publishing Ltd.
P.O. Box 151,
Harrow,
Middx.
HA3 0DH
ENGLAND

Tel: (01) 904 6263

ISBN 0 946719 055

Parts of the text were originally published in February 1986 by Pascal Bussy under the title *The Can Book* through his own Tago Mago label in Paris, France.

A Serious Art Forms production

Printed in England by: The Eastern Press Ltd, Reading, Berks

The Can Book

Concept & direction: Pascal Bussy

Research & interviews: Pascal Bussy & Andy Hall

Contributors: Steven Baker, Mick Fish
Design & layout: Dave Hallbery

CONTENTS

INTRODUCTION

CAN IS BOTH A MAGICAL AND SIGNIFICANT NAME TO many followers of contemporary music. Rarely in modern culture have a group of musicians generated such power and such paradox, achieving a whole universe of creation, matched in its variety only by its density. During the decade from 1968 to 1978, Can teased and provoked the boundaries of musical dogma, inventing and discovering sounds that were as new as they were unique, in a spirit that placed them at the forefront of a true avant-garde.

Now, many years later, this spirit is kept alive in the hearts and dreams of many people, not to mention the late '80s reunion which reactivated it.

"Can have always been a very special band, the perfect link between pop and the avant-garde — the most influential musical force to have come out of Continental Europe, the best example of a group ahead of its time", the English journalist David Elliott summed up in *Sounds* (February 9th, 1985). "They are more original than it is possible to be", another critic once wrote. He was obviously impressed and intrigued by a band whose very lack of formula allowed them to formulate and manifest their music with rhythms, melodies and atmospheres that could be beautiful, brutal, majestic, crude, sinister, transcendental — as limited in dimension only as the listener's own imagination.

The music defies description yet begs it, and the key to any definition of it lies in the spontaneity in which it was conceived. The area in which Can operate in any given time may be rock, blues, hard rock, jazz, experimental, or ethnic music, or a permutation of these — but their own sound is immediately recognisable.

At the beginning of the '70s, Can were the victims of many misinterpretations. They were often compared to Hawkwind and Pink Floyd, and to the German so-called 'cosmic rock' bands, and so on. They were all absurd labels, restricting as they were inexact. Retrospectively, we can see that even with other strong musical personalities (like Kraftwerk, Faust, and maybe Amon Düül II and Guru Guru), the so- called German rock scene never really existed as an entity.

Only a very few comparisons were legitimate. The Velvet Underground (*Yoo Doo Right* and *Sister Ray* possess a close spirit), the energy of the Californian 'acid rock' groups of the '60s, and the early material by Jimi Hendrix and Frank Zappa, are perhaps better comparisons. If such parallels are to be made, they need to be with those individuals and outfits with whom Can share the same energy; James Brown, the Velvet Underground, John Coltrane, the mysterious African voodoo combos...

Hand in hand with the music goes the philosophy of Can, an ideal as well as a band, which as such, has ground rules. On a spiritual level these involve striving with integrity for artistic purity, an openness at all times to the other members of the band, which involves listening intently to what the unit as a whole are producing rather than just playing 'solos'. On a political level, being a true collective in every way — decisions about the music itself, finances, and so on, but also in life-style and attitude (e.g. toward the mechanisms of the music business), that there be an awareness and sensitivity toward the other musicians, their environment, and, by extension, the public.

On top of all this stands the foundation of Can's principle, that of 'instant composition' — an interaction within the group often termed by fans and band alike as 'telepathic'. This method innevitably meant risk-taking, but the results of such collective compositions were never less than exciting, producing a 'possible' (or sometimes seemingly 'impossible') music.

Their attitude toward risk-taking meant that they produced music that was never static, always keen to move on and surprise the listener. Each record Can released always had some elements to disconcert the old fans. *Future Days* by its polished atmosphere, *Soon Over Babaluma* by its exotic feelings, *Landed* by its new sound, *Flow Motion* by its reggae ambiences, and so on.

When they began, the common ground on which they met was clear — each wanted to change his life generally and specifically with regard to the music he was involved in making. Equally clearly, Can were pioneers. They never reached an enormous audience, but their reputation is still growing as the years pass. Their solo careers (as well as new collaborations together or with others) continue to prove that they can still innovate and surprise. Obviously, Can were unable to build up the world-wide reputation that responded to their undoubted talent. This certainly has something to do with the fact that Can never had any special commercial or business strategy, and that their main goal has always been, beside and inside their musical activities, to find a pleasant and happy way of life. It is this art of living which has been their only real ambition, and which each of them has virtually achieved.

Can never followed fashions, but always preceded them. They were the first to explore possibilities of ethno-rock collages, years before the rise of interest in reggae and

Pan-African music. Certainly, they anticipated the popular interest in so-called "world music", bringing extra-European elements into their works, including philosophical influences like Taoism from ancient China. In the late '70s they were also responsible for inspiring many of the New Wave musicians. John Lydon, Cabaret Voltaire, Pete Shelley, The Fall, Wire, The Stranglers, Julian Cope, Siouxsie, the defunct This Heat, and the members of DAF, to name but a few, all cited Can as a major influence. Others, including David Byrne and Eurythmics, owe a lot to them stylistically.

Lastly, they have established a large group of hardcore fans including many people from within the music industry and the rock business, from artists to people working in record company offices in Europe, America and Japan. They have also remained a favourite of many journalists in the music press, almost to the extent of being a 'fetish' interest.

Then of course there are always the myths and legends, and the fascination. This book is not intended as a nostalgic exercise for still grieving fans, but rather a collection of documents about this unique group and their career, giving the ardent Can follower something to chew, as well as being of interest to a newer generation. It cannot replace the music, but it is its evident complement.

Can is from beyond — the magic exists still, defies ageing and dating, to echo around and influence as freshly as ever.

Can is timeless... Enjoy!

HOLGER CZUKAY

Holger Czukay was born on March 24th, 1938 in Danzig, now part of Poland. After the war his family fled to West Germany. His dream as a small boy was to become an organist and a conductor. As a schoolboy, he learnt to repair radios and televisions.

In 1960, he was disqualified from a jazz festival for amateurs, an event that Holger describes by saying, "The jury could not classify my music." Then, in 1962 he learned the double bass under the direction of Mr Zepperitz, the soloist from the Berlin Philharmonic Orchestra, but in the same year he was expelled from the Berlin Music Academy.

After that he went on to study composition with Karlheinz Stockhausen in Darmstadt (Darmstädter Kursen für Neue Musik). Stockhausen was to become one of his biggest musical influences, and to this day they are still in touch with each other. Holger Czukay:

> "I learned a lot of things from my classical studies, and at first when Can began, I thought I was entering into another world. Today, I see the bridge between the two worlds, I see the continuity."

However, Czukay was not entirely happy within Stockhausen's world of the academic avant-garde. It seemed to him that reading every note and instruction from a musical score lacked spontaneity and killed any natural rhythm, and for him any music without a spontaneous rhythm was unnatural. The classical avant-garde music seemed to come far too much from the head and not enough from the body. But what he did learn from Stockhausen was the importance of hard work and a seriousness of purpose. Stockhausen insisted on being personally responsible for

Holger Czukay began experimenting with radio at the age of 14.

every tone in the music, a facet that was to later become important in both Can and Czukay's solo recordings.

Around this time in 1965, at weekends, he would play guitar and accordion with the Jetliners, a dance music trio. He also composed some orchestral scores which remain unpublished to this day. In 1966, he finished his study of serial music and began teaching music classes of his own. While living in Switzerland he became friendly with the conductor of the Mannesmann Symphony Orchestra, who invited him to try his hand at conducting, and to perform one of his own pieces.

Facing the orchestra he dramatically raised the baton and equally dramatically brought it down. Unfortunately, nothing happened until his friend whispered in his ear, "You must draw a deep breath as you raise your hands and expel it violently as you lower them, otherwise they don't think you mean it." Having eventually got the composition underway he became engrossed in the technical problems of conducting, eventually noticing a gradual loss in volume. On looking up he perceived that all but 3 members of the strings, and the brass had beat a strategic retreat. Thus ended his conducting career.

By this time he had developed a bit of a reputation, and the school at St. Gallen insisted upon his services. At the school he was greeted by the Director who noted his credentials, "So, you have no papers, no licence to teach — can you start right away?" Holger Czukay:

"There, my students made me discover rock music. One of my students was Michael Karoli, and together we explored the technical possibilities of the guitar and the modern methods of composition".

Karoli suggested to Czukay that The Beatles were more

"Inability is often the mother of restriction, and restriction is the great mother of inventive performance."

interesting than Stockhausen, and by playing him pieces like *I am the Walrus*, a whole new world of possibilities opened up for Czukay.

At the beginning of the summer of 1968, Holger replied to Irmin Schmidt and David Johnson who wanted him to join them in starting a group. He became the sound-engineer and the bass player of the band, "I chose bass guitar because I thought that nobody listened very carefully to it!" He went on to develop his own very unique bass guitar style, being both minimal and percussive. Holger Czukay:

"When we began Can, Jaki often asked me why I played so much. He would tell me to play only in one tone, that was enough. For me, that was new, and I thought, is only one tone enough, really? To be simple was for me a completely new idea, and simplicity was very difficult.

So, I became a very simple bass player. I never wanted to become a brilliant bass soloist. I considered my way of playing as a sort of summary of everything done by others. I had to find the bass tone of a 'global sound', that was my conception. When I changed anything, that was only to suggest another direction. But I always played the minimum.

Sometimes, what I wanted to achieve with the bass was to only get involved harmonically with it. Every bass player would probably say that. For example, *Bel Air*, is where the bass and the rest of the musicians have a kind of symphonic feeling. I love it when Can gets this symphonic feeling that *Bel Air* has. It's when Micky and Irmin are just getting somewhere, and I put the counterpoint to it. That is something I like and which Jack Bruce

"I became a very simple bass player. I never wanted to become a brilliant bass soloist."

did so well with Cream when they played live. He really found the counterpoint with Clapton. Or like on *Yoo Doo Right*, where it has an absolute African feel of mysticism — very important! And there is something especially mystical about the double bass so that when I play it everyone listens more carefully. Like it had a very good effect on *Red Hot Indians*."

It was this distinctive single tone, or sometimes two note bass lines that provided a perfect counterpoint to Liebezeit's subtlely repetitive drumming, and this minimal and untechnical approach to the whole rhythm section of Can was often the key to the hypnotic power behind a lot of the music. All the members of the group, and Czukay in particular, always made a point of restricting themselves on their respective instruments. Holger Czukay:

"Inability is often the mother of restriction, and restriction is the great mother of inventive performance. For example, Jaki is a fantastic drummer technically, and maybe he is the most technically advanced of the group. But for me, that doesn't mean anything anymore. I'm completely out of that kind of artificial thinking. After Stockhausen, that was finished.

That's why I liked it so much when Jaki was playing saxophone, there was this kind of feeling that there was someone playing who just didn't really know the instrument, but he restricted himself only to what he could do at that moment, and it was very powerful. This is why the saxophone on *Red Hot Indians* is great at the beginning. It is that sort of restriction which gives you power, and it works if you're conscious about that...

For instance, in Japanese music, if you listen to how they restrict themselves — that's the reason they get such a power out of it. Like in Gagaku or Zen music. It is unbelievable, Zen

"Listening through the feet is far better than listening through the ears."

music it really knocks you out. And that 'knocking out' is the feeling we've got to aim for."

However, prior to the advent of punk and the New Wave in 1976, when musical inability became acceptable, the idea of rock musicians trying to limit themselves technically was an unusual standpoint to take. But when musical barriers were redefined in the late '70s a lot of the musicians looked to groups like Can and the Velvet Undergound as a reference point of a more 'non-musical' approach. Mal, the bass player and singer with Cabaret Voltaire:

"At times with Can, both the music and the vocals were restrained, I think they held themselves back. With Holger's bass playing it was always the gaps that interested me."

In 1969, Czukay released the LP *Canaxis 5* with Rolf Dammers. It comprised of some tapes of ethnic music collages mixed with Czukay's bass playing. Holger Czukay:

"I met Rolf during my studies with Stockhausen, he was a musician as well as a great painter, a very sensible person. The whole concept came from both of us. In fact, when I listen to *Canaxis 5* today, I wonder if the original ethnic music is not better than what we did with it..."

The LP was first released on the small Music Factory label from Munich, under the exact reference Schiesshouse Records Production/SRS 002. The two titles were *Ho-Mai-Nhi (Boat Woman Song)* on side one, and *Shock Eyes Ammunition* on side two, both written by Holger Czukay and Rolf Dammers. A short text was included on the back cover:

"Canaxis 5 was written in the light year 77, sometimes called the year of Galactical Score Expedition. Time elapsed between the first founding of the lunar calendar with man's first cough on the moon cow settlement. Leaving behind a flag that waved in a strong moon storm! Plastic man turned himself around on the planet of the moon, trying to reach Canaxis 5. Which is the galaxy of the sound expedition? It was lightning's stroke procedure onto a 45 track recorder, engineered by the robots Ho and Ro. Their laboratory was a stationary space with an orbit outside of the planet KO-V' produced with better sound equipment which was connected electronically with the Inner Space Productions Sound Space Team in a little village in Vietnam. There you can find a secret computer centre of all greater kinds of coloured lightnings."

(*Canaxis 5* was re-released in 1982 on Spoon Records.)

After 8 years as Can's bass player Czukay changed his role within the group and Rosko Gee (formerly of Traffic) replaced Czukay on bass in the Autumn of 1976. Czukay continued to experiment within the group using a short wave radio, telephone, tape recorders, and a guitar with acupuncture needles, a very special device he had used a long time ago on *Yoo Doo Right*. But his role within the group was to become an increasingly uneasy one and he was to leave Can in 1977, just a few months later.

In the same year as he left Can, he took part in a recording with the duo Cluster, a collaboration which was to be renewed the following year with the addition of Brian Eno. Holger Czukay:

"I don't know Cluster very well. It just happened that I was there when they were working in Conny Plank's studio. But they are musicians who try to do something different and they have my interest".

In 1979 he released his critically acclaimed solo LP, *Movies*, on which he had worked since 1977. In Britain the LP was voted a top-five album in the New Musical Express critics poll, and in the same year Czukay was voted Musician of the Year in Germany. Holger Czukay:

"I composed it with the same technique as a film editor would for a movie. The already mixed down music is cut down into 'bits' and spliced together again, as a computer does. The result is something which did not exist before. Computed, or better 'composed' music.

I began the early recording at home with a cassette recorder. Then I used a tape recorder, then three tape recorders. Then, when I prepared the definitive tapes, I transferred them onto the 16 track machine and from there onto the computer desk. Most of the work was done at Inner Space and I did the final mix at Conny Plank's studio. Devo and Ultravox were working during the day and I worked with Conny at night.

When I was working on *Movies*, I was often disheartened, but I received a lot of encouragement from other people; John Foxx,

Dave Stewart and Annie Lennox of Eurythmics, and of course, Conny Plank."

Annie Lennox and Dave Stewart knew Holger Czukay from the time that they visited the Inner Space with their old group The Tourists. Holger, along with Jaki Liebezeit and Robert Gorl from DAF, appeared on Eurythmics first LP in 1981, *In the Garden*. He also appeared with the group on *The Old Grey Whistle Test* TV programme in the same year.

Movies is almost a jigsaw puzzle of sound, culled from a wide variety of sound sources, and all held together by Liebezeit's drumming. Holger Czukay:

"Sometimes I feel like Bryan Ferry - flamboyant!"

Holger Czukay with his favourite instrument - the French horn.

"On *Cool in the Pool* I used cuts from the broadcasts of three radio stations; Radio Luxemburg, Radio France, and one from Russia. For *Oh Lord Give Us More Money* I used some ground tapes from *Landed*. On *Persian Love* (a piece that went on to be used for a Japanese TV commercial for whiskey) I stole the voice of an Iranian poet through my short-wave radio. On *Hollywood Symphony* I made a few winks to Diana Ross. In total for the LP I used many thousands of hours of music. Sometimes I recorded many hours and I only kept a few seconds of, for example, a Korean Orchestra... In the end, Jaki did the drums in two weeks, we worked together in a very secret way that I cannot reveal, but Jaki was able to synchronise himself with the 'orchestra', while I was 'conducting' from the desk - all done spontaneously — Jaki was a fantastic partner.

For *Movies*, and my other solo albums, the recording would be absolutely unusual for any sound engineer. I think that if I would ask the recording machine to buy me coffee, it would do it!"

Czukay assembled his album *Movies* with pieces of tape in the same way other musicians would assemble a composition with notes. With endless editing and thousands of cuts Czukay remodelled all the snippets into the fabric of a composition. (By the late 1980s it was a technique that had become increasingly commonplace with many groups using the computerised 'sampling' of sounds and instruments, particularly on dance and rap records — but was virtually unheard of in 1979). By the use of recorded tapes Czukay could play every instrument if he wanted to, as well as make all musical and technical decisions. "Most musicians have only two hands. Tapes give me hundreds of hands", he told Duncan Fallowell in an interview with *Zig Zag* magazine soon after the release of *Movies*.

Movies still stands today as a remarkable and influential LP. David Sylvian:

"I think it was in 1980 that I was first introduced to Holger's work via the album *Movies*. As with most things in my life that I finally come to love, my initial reaction to the music was negative. But after repeated playing, I grew to know that record inside out and it remains for me today one of the most important 'pop/rock' records ever made. An opinion which, after meeting and working with Holger, understanding his recording techniques, and so on, has been further reinforced."

In 1981, Czukay released his solo LP, *On the Way To The Peak Of Normal*, he also worked on the cult album by the Japanese female singer Phew, which was co-produced with Jaki Liebezeit, Conny Plank, Yoshitaka Goto, and Phew herself. The LP was only released in Japan but he is still in contact with her and he hopes to work with her again. He also played on sessions by Phantom Band and Eurythmics, and co-produced the last two LPs by the Dusseldorf group

"Most musicians have only two hands - tapes give me hundreds of hands."

S.Y.P.H., *Pst* and *Syph*. In 1983 he worked with the German group Trio and in 1984 released a solo LP entitled *The East Is Red*. At the end of 1984, he played two concerts, one in Cologne with Michael Karoli, Jaki Liebezeit and Jah Wobble, and the other in Berlin with Michael Karoli and Jaki Liebezeit. Holger Czukay:

"That was quite interesting. Live you don't have that control that you have in the studio. Everything in the studio can be manipulated, live it's such a different thing. When it's played spontaneously, having some good parts and of course some bad parts in it, then you are able afterwards by editing and recording to bring a powerful form out of it, which makes a lot of sense. That's what I have tended to do.

I did three concerts and I wasn't so satisfied with them as such, but I could imagine that the next album or recordings could come out of a rehearsal or stage appearance and then I could work them out later studiowise. That makes a lot of sense. I heard about the last Talking Heads album, *Naked Ape*, that they have done something like that, just spontaneously playing and later working on it, exactly what I'm doing or did before. Besides I know them, especially Jerry Harrison, I met him twice, he is a very nice guy."

Czukay had met Jah Wobble through Alan Banks of *Rockpalast* who played him a record by Public Image Limited. After listening to the record Czukay said that he would like to meet the group. John Lydon wasn't interested but Jah Wobble was, and the duo of Wobble and Czukay were soon recording an EP together. Jah Wobble's work with Czukay prompted Wobble to comment that, "I will never be as creative as Holger Czukay."

In 1984 and 1985, Czukay played on two successive LPs by David Sylvian, *Brilliant Trees* and *Gone To Earth*. In 1985 he recorded a single called *Hey Baba Rebop*, a piece which he describes as:

"A swing number from the 'swing and stomp' orchestras of the forties, packed into the sound of the eighties. It took me a long time to compose that piece but it was played very easily and fast. This work got me access to new software even though I don't have a computer."

The same year he completed an album called *Rome Remains Rome*, which again featured Jah Wobble on two tracks, as well as Pope Star's Karol Wojtila on lead vocals on the track *Blessed Easter*. He also made several appearances on German television as well as going to Brazil to give workshop lessons for some musicians there.

In August 1987 he produced the excellent *Charlatan* album

by Arno, the Belgian singer from the now defunct TC-Matic. Holger Czukay:

"I am a bit angry with him because he went back to Belgium and he changed the original mix that we had done and which was more powerful. But anyway, working with him was a pleasure. You know, most of these meetings come by chance, sometimes through friends. Arno knew and liked Can from a long time ago."

In 1988 Czukay renewed his working relationship with David Sylvian and the duo recorded two LPs of atmospheric 3D music, the first one being *Plight and Premonition*, followed by *Flux — Mutability*, both albums consisting of two long pieces. The music is based on the environment created by tape and guitar loops and is described by the two as having a filmic quality. On *Flux* several other musicians are involved; Jaki Liebezeit, Michael Karoli, as well as Michy and Markus Stockhausen, who plays flugelhorn.

His work with David Sylvian is very important to him, Holger Czukay often describes him as the person he would most like to work with in the future.

The respect for each other is mutual. David Sylvian:

"On a bright afternoon in 1983, Holger arrived at Hansatone studio, Berlin, where I was recording my first solo album, *Brilliant Trees*. We hadn't met or spoken together before this moment. Smiling, we shook hands and exchanged pleasantries. At a loss for something to say, I asked Holger if he would like to meet the other musicians who were then rehearsing new material upstairs in Studio 2. "First", he said, "I would like to make you a cup of tea". We became very good friends."

By the end of 1988 he had put the finishing touches to his

new "live studio" album called *Radio Wave Surfer* which also features contributions from Michael Karoli and Jaki Liebezeit, as well as Sheldon Ancel on vocals who was already featured on *Rome Remains Rome*.

For most of the sessions on which he is involved, he plays French horn as well as bass guitar and percussion. He is also fascinated by video which he describes as, "a unique

combination of vision and sound." It is a medium which he likes to use very much — notably on such tracks as *Cool in the Pool* and *The Photo Song*.

During 1988 he made the video musical *Krieg der Töne* which was broadcast on German TV on the ZDF channel on April 19th at 10.55 pm. Much of it was filmed in his studio, and he stars as an eccentric who is called to give piano lessons to a young girl by her mother. Holger Czukay:

> "I played a main role together with a 12 year old girl, I also composed the music for the movie. Because of that film, of which some parts were broadcast on Spanish TV as well, I was invited in December '88 to Trento in Italy for a film festival where I met Enio Morricone."

At the beginning of 1989 he flew again to Italy to show his videos and the film at the Bari festival. In Spring 1989 he started work on his upcoming album called *Rhythms Of A Secret Life*, where whales will appear as lead and chorus singers. After this, he wants to write a book, and he is already working with Conny Plank's wife on a fairy tale which will be set to music like a sound filmstory. Holger Czukay:

> "My solo career is my private passion — somehow it's my life and I'm in a fortunate situation — I don't need to do something for money, I can make all that just for fun and for the perspective it will give to me... All my life has been like that. I'm not rich, but my capital is my fantasy. I don't need commercial success, if the record company needs it that's fine, but for me I always accept the feedback I get.
>
> I'm not looking for spectacular success, where you might sell for six months, get one peak and then nothing. I personally prefer to sell constantly, all my life, it keeps me alive, like the

Movies album which is now ten years old and which still sells perfectly well, every year. That's something which is also true for Can, of course - the old albums still sell from the early beginning and that keeps the group alive, that really means something these days and that's the kind of success I prefer."

He is undoubtedly known for his studio wizardry, describing himself as a 'private philharmonist' or in German, 'ein Privatsymphoniker', he has also been known to describe himself as an 'acoustic landscape painter'. David Sylvian:

"Of all the people I've worked with, Holger's compositional recording and editing techniques are the most idiosyncratic. He truly uses the studio as others only profess to; as a compositional tool, an instrument in itself."

Holger Czukay
at the Outer
Space studio
in May 1988.

However, Czukay holds a reserved attitude toward the technology available in the field of recording:

"I love the machines but they must never be boss. Once the machines start to use the composer, the music dies.... People say these machines are a short cut to music but that isn't true at all. Sound effects aren't music, they're just effects. They have to be used."

His musical influences are wide and varied. He is an admirer of the Rolling Stones and especially Keith Richard, (He describes them as "the Volkswagens of rock"). He also admits to having been strongly influenced by dance bands as well as Stockhausen and Lee Perry, who he calls, "a sound master in a musician." He also adds that, "Any music without energy I throw to my tape machine's starving eraserheads."

He lives in the heart of Cologne and is often portrayed as a colourful character, he admits himself that, "Sometimes I feel like Bryan Ferry — flamboyant". His whimsical and unique approach to his music is often punctuated with statements such as "Music and silence are indivisible", or, "Electrons are musical", but can also be tempered with such comments like, "The simplicity of a human being is rare and holy to me", or the conciseness of such observations as, "Politics eats music alive".

Michael Karoli

BORN IN STRAUBING (BAVARIA) ON APRIL 29TH, 1948, Michael Karoli's first instrument in infancy was a tin drum. He then took flute lessons at the age of 4, and piano lessons at 6. Soon his teacher advised him to lay off the piano lessons and take violin lessons instead. This he did at the age of 7, after his grandfather died in Rumania and left him his gypsy violin.

At this time, his musical loves were Mozart, gypsy music, and samba. At the age of ten he tried to build himself a banjo, but finally he was given a tenor banjo for Christmas. This led to him playing dixieland in the school band, the Steamboat

Jazz Pirates, but he was kicked out because the law didn't allow him to play gigs at his age.

At the age of 13 he started to play the guitar, in an attempt to combine the possibilities of the violin and banjo. Soon afterwards, he was given a tape recorder and discovered his liking for overdubbing and distortion.

At this time he mainly listened to piano players like Jelly Roll Morton, Fats Waller, Clarence Williams and Thelonious Monk, along with blues musicians like Big Bill Broonzy, John Lee Hooker and Bessie Smith. He also had a love for the music of Bix Beiderbecke, Louis Armstrong, and the early material of Billie Holiday.

He stopped attending violin lessons at the age of 15 and bought an electric guitar, while at the same time he was given an amplifier from an understanding uncle. He went on to play modern jazz in his school band, and slowly got into Phil Spector, Tamla Motown, English rock 'n' roll, and later more seriously into soul and exotic music. He then left for Switzerland to continue his studies where he sat in with any band he could, playing anything from avant-garde jazz to rock 'n' roll, jamming with Tony Ashton, Remo Four, and

Michael Karoli in summer 1974, during the *Soon Over Babaluma* sessions.

33

"Michael plays the guitar in a weird spidery chip-chop sort of way, quite unlike anyone else."
Duncan Fallowell

many others.

In 1966, through his studies, he met Holger Czukay who showed him 'some tricks' on the guitar and opened his ears to contemporary classical music, while Karoli opened Czukay's ears to some of the pop music of the time. However, in Spring 1967, he left Switzerland and went back to Germany to try and study law as a 'serious' profession, but spent most of his time involved in music, including playing bass in various dance bands in Geneva.

When Michael Karoli was a student he studied planetary

rhythms and the parallels of colours and tones. He tried to develop certain mathematical relationships, comparing the tonic, sub-dominant and dominant with the distance of the earth from Mars, Jupiter and Saturn, and trying to find a word formula for music. To this day, he has a keen interest in astrology and has several times sought guidance from this area with regard to critical decisions in his life.

He met up with Holger Czukay again in 1968 and they worked together on a project that attempted to merge free jazz, rock, contemporary classical music and ethnic music into a new type of music. Holger Czukay then introduced him to Irmin Schmidt, a Kapellmeister and composer in Cologne, who wanted to form a band that encapsulated the same spirit and had asked Holger Czukay to join.

Within this group that became Can, Michael Karoli developed a very personal way of playing guitar, avoiding cliches and routine. "Michael plays the guitar in a weird spidery chip-chop sort of way, quite unlike anyone else." Duncan Fallowell comments on the cover notes to *Tago Mago*. His style was a melding of rock, folk and gypsy themes that became a unique corner-stone to the group's music. As John Gill wrote, "A guitar that could change from sounding like a car crash to a solo sax to a choirboy in one song..." It was also a guitar style that was not only very original but also to become influential. Pete Shelley of The Buzzcocks commented in 1978, "I would never have played the guitar had it not been for the late Marc Bolan and Michael Karoli of Can."

As well as the guitar, he also played violin and sang on some of Can's material, most notably on *Dizzy Dizzy*. He also sang on Can's early material before Malcolm Mooney's arrival, most of which remains unreleased. He returned to singing with the group between 1974-1978, although he had

always provided backing vocals on a lot of the tracks. He remained the guitarist with Can until the time when the group ceased operations. His only spell of inactivity was due to being taken seriously ill with a perforated ulcer in August of 1972 which put him out of action until the beginning of the following year.

After the members of Can went their own ways in the late '70s, Karoli left Cologne in 1978 to live in France, in the country near Nice, where he built his own studio, the Outer Space. During the summer of 1981, he undertook his first production, the maxi-single by Bits, a Dusseldorf band comprising of ex-members of the group S.Y.P.H. In 1984, he released his own solo album *Deluge* with the English female singer Polly Eltes, an ex-member and co-founder of the all-girl rock 'n' roll revue The Moodies and a successful fashion model in England. (She appeared on the front cover of Roxy Music's LP *Country Life*).

In 1984 and 1985 he worked and prepared new material with various musicians; Polly Eltes, Jaki Liebezeit, several local and African musicians, and a project with the saxophonist Barney Wilen (formerly the successor to John

Michael Karoli
in his garden in
Nice in May
1988.

37

Coltrane in the Miles Davis Quintet) and Georges Ambrosio, a percussionist from Nice. He has also played on most of the film soundtracks and records by Irmin Schmidt as well as playing guitar on *Oh Lord Give Us More Money* on Holger Czukay's *Movies* LP.

He returned to the live stage twice in 1984, once with Jah Wobble and Jaki Liebezeit in Cologne, and the other with two Can members Holger Czukay and Jaki Liebezeit in Berlin. The Berlin concert was sponsored by the programme *Rockpalast* and part of it was shown on German television. "Both concerts were very encouraging," commented Karoli, "and there will certainly be more coming, especially with the Berlin line-up with just the three of us."

From 1985 to 1987, he contributed to various solo recordings by the other members of Can, notably playing guitar and co-writing *Perfect World* on Holger Czukay's *Rome Remains Rome* album. In August 1987 he recorded the *Charlatan* album by the Belgian singer Arno, with Holger Czukay producing. He also plays on Holger's albums *Radio Wave Surfer* and *Rhythms Of The Secret Life*, as well as on the *Flux - Mutability* album by Holger Czukay and David Sylvian. On these last two projects he also shares a composing role. He has also played on nearly all of Irmin Schmidt's projects, including the *Musk At Dusk* and *Reporter* albums.

In 1989 he hopes to finish his own solo record on which he plays guitar and sings as well, with Jaki Liebezeit playing the drums and lyrics by Duncan Fallowell. In 1989, he also became a father to a daughter, Tamara.

JAKI LIEBEZEIT

BORN NEAR DRESDEN IN MAY, 1938. JAKI LIEBEZEIT WAS brought up in a musical family and very soon learned to play the piano and trumpet. He sang and played trumpet in his school band, and later the horn in the school's brass band. At 18, he became the drummer in his high school band in Kassel, where he met the jazz trumpeter Manfred Schoof.

After exploring many different musical directions, he settled in Cologne where he played in a jazz band with Schoof and other musicians like Gunter Hampel, Olaf Kübler, and Lothar Meid. His first concert was in Munich with Olaf Kübler (sax) and Buschi Niebergall (bass).

From 1961 to 1965 he lived in Spain working in a jazz club in Barcelona. Amongst others, he played with the trumpeter Chet Baker and the pianist Tete Montoliu, and also discovered Spanish and Latin rhythms. In 1966, he joined the Manfred Schoof Quintet, which also included Gerd Dudek (sax), Alex von Schlippenbach (piano), and Buschi Niebergall. He stayed with this group for two years, who were at this time one of the most influential bands of the new European jazz scene. (A few records from this period are available on the German labels; Free Music Production, L & R Records, and Wergo). However, he was generally disappointed with their music. Jaki Liebezeit:

> "It was the great period of free jazz, everyone wanted to destroy the old schemes, but some musicians took it to the extreme and by refusing harmonies and simple rhythms they destroyed everything. At the end I was not happy in the group."

On his second visit to Spain, Jaki Liebezeit joined a quartet which included a Cuban bass player, who doubled as the support act, playing solo. Jaki was impressed with the way that the Cuban played seemingly simple themes but embellishing them with his own style. This never failed to get the audience going, and somebody explained to Jaki that the Cuban had some very secret rhythms which he wouldn't tell anyone about. This person also suggested to Jaki that somebody should find out more about them. This Jaki did, but also uncovered a macabre story in the process.

The bassist had apparently played with a fellow Cuban drummer, Chano Pozo, several years before. Pozo had learnt many secret voodoo rhythms, and against his better judgement insisted on playing these to people, despite being absolutely forbidden to by a voodoo sect. The Cuban paid the full penalty by being executed on stage during one of these

Jaki Liebezeit
in 1970, during
the *Tago Mago*
sessions.

performances. Jaki Liebezeit:

> "It is something that I heard, I did not witness the actual execution."

However, later Irmin Schmidt added further to the mystery by saying:

> "There are some secret Can rhythms, and if anyone plays them to the public they will be executed, but that's another story!"

At this time Liebezeit vaguely knew Irmin Schmidt, who

had attended a few concerts by the Manfred Schoof Quintet. Later, the two developed an association when they worked on a score for the film *We Two*, although his brilliantly conceived drum solo derived from automobile noises is cut from the final soundtrack. One day Schmidt called him up to ask for his advice in finding a drummer, but Schmidt had no need to look any further, as Liebezeit answered the call himself immediately becoming the drummer of the group.

His drumming style developed after he spent a long time studying ethnic music, "These tabla players who create a strong tension by not playing a beat, that is something we've always looked for." It was this style, based on repetition and played on his legendary blue Sonor drum kit, which at once became one of the main distinctive features of the Can sound. Jean-Noël Ogouz, former label manager at United Artists in France:

"I've been impressed by two drummers in rock music who had very personal styles; the drummer of Redbone, and the drummer of Can, two very different styles, though, of course."

It was a metronomic style that provided a welcome change from many of the flamboyant drumming styles prevalent in rock music at the time. However, like Can many of the German bands that started in the '70s were to use the same repetitive approach towards rhythm. Mal from Cabaret Voltaire:

"Can were the most exotic of the German bands, they were a lot less technical than Kraftwerk or Neu. The cyclic drumming and reggae-ish feel to the music seemed to marry the Germanic and ethnic elements perfectly.

Jaki Liebezeit and the whole rhythmic side to the music was the biggest influence on me. After listening to Can's records, for a long time I wanted to be a drummer, but I soon realised I wasn't that well co-ordinated!"

As well as his liking for, and affinity with ethnic music, Liebezeit's style of playing also developed from his increasing disillusionment with free jazz. Jaki Liebezeit:

"When Can began I really wanted to get as far away from free jazz as possible. In free jazz there is no real rhythm, no harmonic rhythm. Once somebody - some kind of freak - came up to me when I was playing free jazz and said, "Why do you play that shit? You must play monotonously." I thought he was crazy! "You must play monotonously." I still have it in my mind, I know he was right. It seemed that everyone related 'monotonous' with 'bad'. But this meant that there are some people who like it."

Later, during the early Malcolm Mooney period of Can, this concept of 'monotony' was explored in great depth, and there was a conscious effort by the group to keep colour out of their music. It was this that inspired Malcolm Mooney to sing the words, "any colour's bad", on *Outside My Door*. Jaki Liebezeit:

"I think I could play anywhere in the world because I can understand the rhythms they play there. They are all the same, they play a 3/4, a 4/4, it's based on symmetry. A tabla doesn't sound like a snare drum but the music is the same.

All the rhythms I play are natural. Sometimes people would start clapping when we played *One More Night* or *Splash*, although they didn't understand the rhythm. They didn't realise that it's a 7/8 rhythm. They hear the punctuation between, and beyond that they are not interested. They just get the basic movements.

"When Can began I really wanted to get as far away from free jazz as possible."

I think you can play any rhythm, 5/8, 7/8, 8/8, 3/8, anything, so long as you get the basic movements. 7/8 is as simple as 8/8. Some musicians cannot play it, but that's because they're not used to it. You only have to go 500 kilometres to Czechoslovakia, Hungary, Yugoslavia, Rumania, Greece, Turkey and so on, and any dance band will play like that. They can play all these rhythms with the same simplicity that musicians play a waltz or a march here. If you go too high like 13/8 it starts to get a little complicated. But you can divide it so that the tempo is slow until 13 beats have passed from 1 to 1. So you make it such that people don't think there are thirteen beats in between."

As well as drumming Jaki Liebezeit also played some wind instruments with Can. Although he likes a lot of different music, including a wide variety of ethnic music, he rarely listens to records.

Outside of Can, he has played with many musicians, including Brian Eno, Joachim Witt and Michael Rother. He has also played on most of Holger Czukay's records and productions, as well as the sessions with Jah Wobble. He has also contributed to nearly all the Irmin Schmidt film soundtracks, as well as playing with the Eurythmics, Plaza Hotel, and Gabi Delgado. He attaches a great importance to his contribution to the LP by the Japanese singer Phew, on which he was the drummer, co-composer and the co-producer. Jaki Liebezeit:

> "It was a unique and absolutely non-commercial thing, like the old Can. She arrived, nothing was written except maybe a few sentences, and we all made the music spontaneously in the

"The bass guitar is a stupid instrument, I really don't like it, it's like a dinosaur."

"These tabla players who create a strong tension by not playing a beat, that is something we have always looked for."

studio. Phew is really someone, she is not the everyday pop singer, she's not a Yoko Ono, she's just Phew, a strange person from Japan."

Just after the disbanding of Can, he started his own group called Phantom Band which released three albums, (*Phantom Band*, *Freedom of Speech* and *Nowhere*). The group also played a few concerts. He was a close friend of the late famous German producer Conny Plank, who regarded him as the best drummer in modern music. Plank took him to Italy to play on a Gianna Mannini LP. Jaki Liebezeit:

"When I do these kinds of commercial studio sessions I don't do it only for money, I must have an understanding with the people. If it works, I can play anything they want, it's their style then. As long as we come to a common basis everything is OK."

In 1986, Jaki began to participate in the Damo Suzuki Band project. Jaki Liebezeit:

"It is basically the same thing as Phantom Band. The guitar player is the same, the keyboard player is a friend of the Phantom Band keyboard player, and I am there. Both Damo and I are quite well known in Germany and we get quite a lot of live gigs there."

On September 27th, 1987, Jaki Liebezeit and Rosko Gee ("from Can", according to the bill) played with Julian Dawson and the Flood at London's Ronnie Scott Club in Soho.

In 1989, Jaki Liebezeit doesn't think that his approach to the drums has changed that much:

"Maybe the sound has changed, but basically it's the same - the beat is like an old thing, going back to before the music of the Middle-Ages. You can still hear it in a primitive way in India or in Turkey, in all these countries where non-written music is played, it's based on a certain key, you have to stay within a few notes and not add any other. In pop music it's the same but the sound is different, you keep the key and the rhythm structure, and the chords which are there."

He is also considering a new solo project. Jaki Liebezeit:

"It should be a non-commercial project. The production of the Phantom Band was very bad because I produced most of the things and I'm not so good at producing records. We couldn't afford a producer, but there were some good ideas. We all learned a lot from the three records and for me it was very important to do that. A pure solo work might come a little bit later. Yes, I might do something solo-wise, maybe a whole record with just drums. For example, in Cologne I know most of the interesting, good drummers and they know me, so sometimes we get together and just play spontaneously, that's something I'd like to develop."

Today, Jaki Liebezeit has an aversion to the bass guitar:

"I don't like this old concept of bass. Why must there be a bass? Most of the bands cannot play without a bass player, it's absurd. The bass guitar is a stupid instrument, I really don't like it, it's

like a dinosaur. Of course, there I'm speaking of the electric bass, this instrument which makes all the stage shake with huge loudspeakers. With the double bass it's different, I like it very much, it's like a big violin, you can bow it and get a lot of nice sounds from it. For many years now, I haven't played with a bass player, except in the studio, of course, but that's something else.

The last bass player I played with on stage was Jah Wobble, but that chapter is finished because we had some trouble, we did some concerts and he was unfriendly towards us, he was maybe too drunk, I don't know... But for example, look at Holger, he doesn't play bass anymore, he is more like a composer now, making music, not playing bass. He uses radios, strange things, his dictaphone, he has found his own way of making music."

Despite this "bomb the bass" syndrome, Jaki Liebezeit has never stopped making music since his first days as a musician, he is constantly working and is busy all the time. He is a master mathematician and his syncopated metallic drumming is more efficient than a drum machine. His metronomic style is still the trade mark of most of the Can members solo works. He has recently moved from Weilerswist, the village where the Inner Space studio is located, to the centre of Cologne where he now lives.

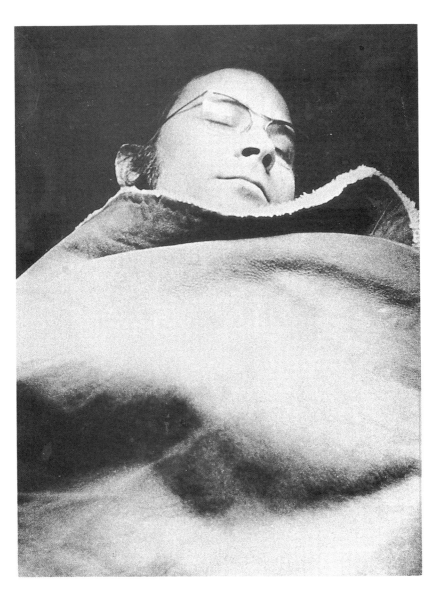

IRMIN SCHMIDT

IRMIN SCHMIDT WAS BORN IN BERLIN ON MAY 29TH, 1937. AS a child he had a beautiful singing voice and his first musical experiences were singing in his school's church choir. He was later expelled from the same school for having organised jazz concerts, and having refused to allow his teacher to play in the youth orchestra he had founded.

From 1957 to 1959, he studied piano and French horn at the Dortmund College of Music and subsequently became a piano teacher. At the Folkwang Akademie of Essen, he continued his piano studies with Ditlis Kraus, and also studied composition and orchestral conducting, obtaining his

Irmin Schmidt
conducting in
Essen in the
early sixties.

degree with the highest possible commendation, and went on to conduct several important orchestras including the Vienna Symphony Orchestra.

Around this time, he first began to take an interest in John Cage, and he played *Winter Music* on piano and conducted *Atlas Eclipticalis*. He would often give chamber music concerts and piano recitals during which he would play compositions by Morton Feldman, Olivier Messiaen, Luigi Nono, and so on, as well as the conventional classical repertoire.

He then went to Salzburg in Austria to continue his conducting studies with Istvan Kertesz, and won the prize for the course. Moving to Cologne he studied at the Kölner Kurse für Neue Musik with Stockhausen, Berio, Pousseur and Brown, and also studied ethnic music at Cologne University. At the same time he studied with Cage, Stockhausen, Boulez and Berio at the Darmstädter Kurse für Neue Musik. In Cologne he met Holger Czukay, Jon Hassel (who lived in his flat), Katrina Klimski, David Johnson, and Serge Tcherepnin.

In 1964 he won the prize of the Bundesauswahl Junger Kunstler and thereby conducted the Hannover Radio Symphony Orchestra. In 1965, for the first time he played with Holger Czukay. Irmin Schmidt:

"Holger was trying to teach me the percussion part of one of his compositions, something absolutely unplayable, a pure piece of mathematics..."

He then became the Kappelmeister at the theatre of Aachen, and a singing teacher at the Bochum Schauspielschule, where he taught his students how to sing Brecht amongst others. He also played on the festival circuit, as pianist, occasional percussionist, and conductor. He also started to compose music for theatre plays, movies, and television; one of these projects was to compose new music for some Brecht pieces after he had met Paul Dessau in East Berlin.

In January 1966, he went to New York for the Mitropulos contest, organised for conductors. It is there that he met and played with Terry Riley, La Monte Young, Steve Reich, and also Dick Higgins from the Fluxus group. It was during this contest that Schmidt decided to make a break with classical and contemporary music and abandon his traditional career and turn his musical attentions toward a different direction:

"I have very fond memories of my classical studies, and I have never denied classical music. I had a wonderful time as a conductor, working with musicians as well as playing Mozart or Chopin. Today, I still like to play pieces by Debussy, Chopin and others. It is not that I don't like the music, it is the structure within which people play it - the professional structure that's completely different.

And also I am not just a player, but also a composer, I have very personal needs to express myself, to communicate with the others within the music. I was looking for the feeling to do that. That is how the musicians in Can met. The spontaneity of each of us was the concept and it never stopped."

His first association outside the confines of classical music was with the American composer and flautist David Johnson,

whom he first met during his studies with Stockhausen, and with whom he shared a strong interest in electronic music and free improvisational forms. To found a group, they got in touch with Holger Czukay, and together whilst listening to Jimi Hendrix, Frank Zappa and the Mothers of Invention, and the first album by the Velvet Underground they had the idea of including a rock elements within the group. Irmin Schmidt always felt an affinity toward the Velvet Underground and John Cale in particular, about whom he says, "He's a bit like me, a professional musician, but at heart an overstudied amateur."

Within Can, Schmidt developed a unique way of playing his keyboards, quite unlike the sound produced from a traditional keyboard. This inventive approach could take many forms. The famous South African piano player Abdullah Ibrahim (Dollar Brand) often explains that karate (or "bushido" as he says) plays a significant role in his improvising method. This comment could also apply to

"Blues is a cliché, but you can still make fantastic things out of it."

Irmin Schmidt, as the great inventor of his legendary karate-chop style on his keyboards.

Besides his musical activities Schmidt was very involved in the art world between the years of 1958 to 1968, and had associations with painters as well as assisting with the organisation of exhibitions. Through an association with the famous art critic Schulze Vellinghaus he even became an art critic himself and worked in that capacity for a number of newspapers.

Before Can, Irmin Schmidt worked a lot with theatre music. Through that, he became acquainted with the film music scene in Germany, and it was very natural that Can went on to work in that genre:

"Yes, it was always me that cared about film music for Can. And after Can, I of course continued with it. We worked with everybody in Germany except Herzog and Fassbinder. With *Bottom*, in early 1970, we began to really work around the movie itself, as we did later for *Deep end, Deadlock, Alice in den Städten*, and so on. On *Bottom*, we used for the first time the sound of shortwaves, recording tapes which were directly inspired by the images of the film. And beside Thomas Schamoni, I met Peter Przygodda, who became the most famous film editor in Germany. He now works with Wim Wenders and he influenced me very deeply as a film composer.

I really think that film music is an art in itself and that it gives you ideas for your musical thinking. But much of Can's film music remains unreleased on record, like the one that we did for *Alice in den Städten* for Wim Wenders around 1973/74. In fact, that soundtrack was recorded by only Michael Karoli and me, he was on guitar and I was playing directly on the strings of the grand piano. I once had a very good tape of it but now it is lost."

Since 1980 Schmidt has lived with his wife and daughter in

Provence, France. He has recently built a small studio there, which he has called Studio Rossignols after the name of his house. He has continued to produce numerous film and television soundtracks, four records of which have already been released, and others will be released regularly. *Filmmusik 1* was compiled from various soundtracks recorded between 1978 and 1981, and includes the music from *Messer im Kopf*, the famous Reinhard Hauff movie. On *Filmmusik 2* and *Filmmusik 3 & 4*, most of the members of Can are featured. In 1979 and 1980, he recorded an LP entitled *Toy Planet* with the Swiss saxophonist Bruno Spoerri. Irmin Schmidt:

"It was a solo project which became a duo project. We recorded the LP at Bruno's studio in Zurich. It draws upon myths from all over the world, one of my passions. It's a bit like my Tolkien or my Borges album, a possible soundtrack for fantasies and constructed imaginary culture. All the sounds are electronic apart from the saxophone although, sometimes one thinks one can hear a guitar, some percussion, or even a balalaika and animal screams... The title was invented by Michael Karoli, he offered it to me and then he regretted it!"

In 1981 Schmidt produced an LP by the Swiss guitarist Thomas Diethelm entitled *Shaved*. He also played and recorded a two day session with Reebop at the Inner Space Studio, parts of which appear on *Filmmusik 3 & 4* (*City of Magic, Asagrai*), the rest of the session is as yet unreleased. In 1982 he worked on a composition for symphony orchestra with jazz and rock soloists (Michael Karoli on guitar, John Marshall on drums, Manfred Schoof on trumpet, Trilok Gurtu on percussion), commissioned by Nord Deutscher Rundfunk, and premiered in Hamburg on November 5th.

In 1983, he composed a long soundtrack for ten episodes of

"There is no
Can piece
which is
finished..."

the German television series *Rote Erde*; amongst other
musicians it features Gerd Dudek (soprano saxophone),
Michael Karoli (guitars and bass), Manfred Schoof (trumpet),
Steve Baker (harmonica) and David Johnson (flute). It was
the first time in fifteen years he had played with the pre-Can
member David Johnson. The soundtrack album went on to
be released in Germany.

In 1984 and 1985, he worked on two new television serials
and two theatre commissions (including a play by Heiner
Müller performed in Berlin and Nancy at the Festival des
Nations), plus various film soundtracks, notably *Flight to
Berlin* by Christopher Petit and *Alle Geister Kreisen* by Peter
Przygodda.

He also produced a solo piano album by Katrina Klimski,
called *Ambrosia*. The grand piano remains his favourite
instrument:

"I never had very fashionable equipment. I never had a dozen
keyboards on stage. But all these electronic instruments, I
become quickly tired of. The only instrument I will never tire of

is the grand piano, it is still my favourite instrument and it always will be. All these electronic instruments have a limitation, and they are far from the body. Not so with the grand piano, and it is the same with the guitar, you can influence its sound with all the body."

In 1987 he released his first real solo rock album, *Musk At Dusk*, an attractive album of warm and dreamy exotic pop songs which was recorded in three different locations; the Outer Space Studio near Nice, the Can studio in Weilerswist, the Powerplay Studios near Zürich. The lyrics are by Duncan Fallowell, the ex-journalist who was the first to write an article about Can in an English music paper (*Melody Maker*, October 30th 1971, titled "Can, the heaviest of all?") Fallowell is now a novelist whose most recent book was entitled *Satyrday*, an ironic and powerful chronicle of our times published in 1987 by Paladin Books in London. Irmin Schmidt:

"When I have a song without words I sing it to Duncan and then he writes the lyrics and the whole rhythm changes because I have something to say in the song."

On *Musk At Dusk* Irmin Schmidt's vocalising style is rather special, it's a sort of blending of singing, whispering, and spoken words, and was a style that had already been hinted at with Can on *Come Sta, La Luna* (on the *Soon Over Babaluma* album) and *Babylonian Pearl* (on *Flow Motion*). Irmin Schmidt:

"That's my way of doing it, I feel that without the voice something is missing in this music — the human voice. And if anyone else is singing, it's not my music anymore..."

Musk At Dusk features a main nucleus of musicians with Schmidt on vocals, keyboards and synthesizers, Michael

Karoli on guitars, Jaki Liebezeit on drums, Franck Ema-Otu
on bass guitar, and Trilok Gurtu, with extra guests on a few
pieces like Manfred Schoof on flugelhorn on *Villa Wunderbar*
and *Alcool* and Gerd Dudek on saxophone and Serge Ferrara
on accordion on *Roll on Euphrates*, a piece which was the
main theme for the Schimanski Tatort movie *Freunde*, a
thriller which was made for German TV in 1987.

For a number of years, Schmidt has concentrated mainly on
this eclectic side to his work. He has composed many other
soundtracks for German TV; *Kein Schöner Land* (1985 - four
episodes), *Reporter* which will appear as the main part of the
volume 5 of his *Filmmusik* series (1989 - six episodes), and the
follow up to the *Rote Erde* serial (1990 - four episodes). Irmin
Schmidt:

"These film soundtracks are still a part of my activities and of
course they represent an important part of my income."

He also composed some music for the theatre; *Wallenstein*
by Schiller for the Berlin Theatre (1985), *Victor oder Die Kinder
an der Macht* by Roger Vitrac (from the French *Victor ou Les
Enfants au Pouvoir*). Besides these, Irmin Schmidt started to
work on his first opera in 1988, for one of Germany's most

Irmin Schmidt
at the Outer
Space studio in
May 1988

important publishers of contemporary classical music,
Schott-Söhne in Mainz. Irmin Schmidt:

> "It will not be a rock opera, nor a work à la Luigi Nono, but
> there is one thing I know and that is that the rhythm will be
> strong, and it will also feature a large orchestra. But I don't
> know yet whether I will use traditional drums which don't fit in
> so well with the large orchestra, or percussion, which blends
> better in the symphonic sound.
>
> Anyway, I don't want to do a work for a small elite. I respect
> Stockhausen (there are beautiful moments in *Kontakt* and in the
> opera *Transe*.), Nono, and Philip Glass as well, but in the same
> field I prefer the John Adams opera *Nixon in China*, and some
> works by Steve Reich, like *Music for 18 Musicians*, these pieces
> are easily understandable for a large audience although they are
> very complex, they reflect a phenomenal sense of the sound
> from their composers. In fact, in all the classical music I listen to,
> the ones I prefer are; Messiaen, Nono, Ligeti, Schubert, and my
> favourites are really Debussy and Schumann."

In the rock field, Irmin Schmidt is also working on the
follow up to *Musk At Dusk*. Again, all the lyrics will be by
Duncan Fallowell, and the working title of this new album is
Le Weekend. Irmin Schmidt:

> *Musk At Dusk* was a bit melancholic, this new one will be more
> happy, more aggressive, the role of the lyrics will be very
> important, the whole album will have a literary aspect."

Lastly, Irmin Schmidt has a long term project which
remains a bit secret at the moment. He wants to direct a film.
"All I can say is that it will be related to a certain kind of
music..."

CHRONOLOGY

1968

june

Holger Czukay, David Johnson, Michael Karoli, Jaki Liebezeit and Irmin Schmidt meet in Cologne and start working on material in David Johnson's flat with only one microphone and a Revox tape recorder. The initial line-up consists of; Holger Czukay (bass), David Johnson (flute), Michael Karoli (guitar — also sings), Jaki Liebezeit (drums) and Irmin Schmidt (organ). Irmin Schmidt:

"We began without any concept, our only idea was to find a concept in making music all together spontaneously, in a collective way and without any leader."

A few days later, they are invited by a patron, who they meet through a mutual friend Manni Löhe, who owns a castle (Schloss Norvenich) in a suburb of Cologne to play their first concert in front of an audience especially made up of artists. It is interesting to note that throughout their history Can have often been supported by patrons in the old artistic tradition, from the early Schloss Norvenich days to the brand new album *Rite Time*. At the first concert they play improvisations based on a mixture of wild rock music, ethnic music and collages. David Johnson brings a tape of the Paris riots of May '68, and Holger Czukay some choir music by the Belgian Polyphonist Renaissance composer Pierre de la Rue. Holger Czukay:

"I still have the tape of the first concert, and there is much magic in it. It was the first step, and we were all very excited and nervous. It was the first time that I had played live with electric amplification and loudspeakers! I was on bass and I was in charge of the tapes, as well as David who played flute, Micky was on guitar, Irmin on piano and organ, and Jaki on drums, percussion and flute. Our friend Manni Löhe guested on vocals, percussion and flute."

(Large extracts from this concert have been released on cassette in 1984 on the French label Tago Mago under the name 'Prehistoric Future' — see discography. On January 25th, 1985, the cassette reaches No 2 in the Avant-Garde Top Twenty published in the pop weekly *Sounds*, which was compiled in the same week by Recommended Records in London).

The owner of Schloss Norvenich subsequently agrees to let them use one of the rooms as a studio. They adopt the collective name of Inner Space and begin to rehearse. Holger

Czukay and David Johnson are the sound technicians.

July

E.F.S. No 7, the only studio track so far released from this period has the strong influence of ethnic music. The Albanian wind instrument sound is achieved by a broken clarinet mouthpiece in a broken flute body.

August

Hildegard Schmidt, through Serge Tcherepnin, meets a black sculptor in Paris called Malcolm Mooney, who soon becomes the vocalist of the group. He has no singing experience but when he arrives in the studio he immediately pushes the music more towards rock music as if he was forcing the four Germans to cross a canyon... *Father Cannot Yell* which opens the *Monster Movie* album, is the second take of his first session with Inner Space. David Johnson is the sound engineer but he does not play on the piece.

David Johnson and Holger Czukay rehearsing in the first studio.

November   They record the music for the *Kama Sutra* movie, the only time
            when the six musicians of Inner Space all play together. A
            single with two extracts from these sessions is released in
            Germany, strangely credited to the sole name of Irmin Schmidt.

December   David Johnson decides to leave the band and goes back to
            the free-music world, working in Germany and in the United
            States. (Today, he is the director of the electronic music
            studio at the Basel Academy in Switzerland).
            Jaki Liebezeit and Malcolm Mooney find a new name for the
            band: The Can. The definite article "The" is soon dropped
            from the name between the release of *The Can Soundtracks*
            and *Tago Mago*. (The Turkish word 'can' (pronounced
            "chan") means life or soul, the Japanese word 'kan' means
            feeling or emotion, and the Japanese word 'chan' means love
            when used in salutation).
            A few years later, Irmin Schmidt will take delight in
            declaring to a few journalists that the real meaning of the
            three letters of Can is: Communism, Anarchism, Nihilism...
            In the same vein, he said to the German magazine *Tip*, for a
            retrospective article in 1984, "We were never a normal rock
            group. Can was an anarchist community."

1969

The group record the tracks *The Empress and the Ukraine King* and *E.F.S. No 10*, two early pieces which are indicative of some of the band's different styles.

Get The Can, their most extrovert piece, is recorded live in front of a audience consisting of friends and artists at Norvenich. Holger Czukay includes some snippets from his *Canaxis 5* in the final mix.

March/May   The group record a number of tracks including; *Little Star of*

Bethlehem (also called *Froggie And Toadie*), *De La Halle*, *Million Seller* (later retitled *Connection*), also the first versions of *She Brings The Rain, Outside My Door, Moving Slowly Going Uphill*, and *Mother Upduff* the latter of which is a long session most parts of which remain unreleased. In this last piece Malcolm Mooney tries his hand at the saxophone and then improvises the lyrics from a true story he has read in a paper about a German family on holiday in Italy. During the holiday the grandmother suddenly died and her body was put on the roof-rack of the minibus. While the family was eating somewhere, the grandmother was stolen!

July 25th

Can play a live concert at Norvenich, based on two long performances of *Yoo Doo Right*. An extract appears on the whole of side two of *Monster Movie*. In the middle of the concert one of the two amps blows up but they continue, showing the group's growing acceptance of all the circumstances of an event. At that time the group had a limited number of initial influences. Holger Czukay:

> "We wanted to make something very simple with a lot of repetition. Of course we were aware of the ideas of Terry Riley and others, but we did not look to that. Rather we looked towards the Velvet Underground. They were the first group we had ever heard who were playing something with a completely new relation to their instruments, very unconventional in their way of playing, a magic way. Repetition is like a machine, and of course we like machines. If you can become aware of the life of a machine, then you are definitely a master."

In fact, the feeling of restriction that the group likes so much is never more in evidence than during this Malcolm Mooney era. The group are not only restricted by shortcomings in their individual techniques, but also in their recording equipment. We also hear Malcolm Mooney on saxophone in such pieces as *Mother Upduff*. Holger Czukay:

"In the case of *Yoo Doo Right*, everyone was restricting themselves nearly to zero. There is so much tension created by restriction. Everybody had proved themselves as musicians, although in different fields. Then if you restrict yourself to nearly nothing, just doing the most simple thing in order to find something that everyone has in common, then you feel the power of restriction. Everyone was doing as little as possible and that is what generated the power that the piece has."

August

The group play another concert at Norvenich, this time playing simultaneously with an art exhibition taking place upstairs. Can begin with *Moving Slowly Going Uphill* but the audience movement between the concert and the exhibition distracts Malcolm Mooney who begins to scream, "Upstairs, downstairs." He continues throughout the intermission and the second half and he finally collapses. Michael Karoli:

"It was quite nice really. Malcolm lost his head, which happened sometimes. The atmosphere was really good."

Can release their first LP, *Monster Movie*, on the small Music Factory label from Munich. The original 500 copies sell out within two weeks of release. They sign a contract with United Artists and the LP is re-released on the traditional market.

On the original Music Factory cover the five members were credited as follows: Irmin Schmidt (adminaspace co-ordinator & organ laser), Jaki Liebezeit (propulsion engineer & mystic space chart reader), Holger Czukay (hot from Vietnam; technical laboratory chief & red armed bass), Michael Karoli (sonar & radared guitar pilot), Malcolm

Holger Czukay
and Michael
Karoli.

Mooney (linguistic space communicator).

Irmin Schmidt, who was the least 'rock music' orientated of the group, was the person most unsure of his role within the group in the early days. Irmin Schmidt:

"No, I don't play a lot on *Monster Movie* and on the early pieces, because when it became obvious that Can was, let's say a 'rock group', I was the one that had the least experience in that field, and my work at the beginning was more about giving an instrumental colour, a very orchestral sound. But I don't feel at all that I have a less important role on *Monster Movie* than the others. On all the Can albums there is always one of us who is doing a bit more than the others, but that doesn't mean anything."

September

Can are asked to provide the music for the theatre play *Prometheus* by Heiner Müller, which is to run for three months at the Zurich Schauspielhaus. Just before the première the director abandons his original idea of an equal collaboration between actors and musicians, and asks Can to play discreet background music. They come on stage in an angry mood and Malcolm Mooney screams into his microphone, "Das Schauspielhaus ist Scheisse!" ("The Schauspielhaus is shit!"). Then, they play the loudest they possibly can.

Later they come to an agreement with the theatre management who lets them use the theatre for a one hour free concert after the play itself. Some nights Can attract a larger audience than *Prometheus*. And, for one special evening, they are allowed to give a long concert, from 6.00pm to 1.00am It turns out as a special event called *Can-action-rock-incitement-playground* with people coming on stage, dancing, painting on plastic sheets, etc. A big aluminium can is also on stage. *Die Tat*, a local paper from Zurich, writes:

"These guys are sitting on wooden chairs playing electric instruments, it would be better if they were sitting on electric chairs playing wooden instruments."

(Can use this quote in the future for promotion purposes).

Apart from this unusual beginning to their live career outside of Schloss Norvenich, Can record two pieces in Zurich, in a cellar transformed into an improvised studio. *Fall Of Another Year*, which includes a beautiful out-of-tune flute solo played by Malcolm Mooney, is based on a Brazilian samba, and *The Thief* will be used as the soundtrack of the Spiecker film *Kuckucksei In Gangsternest*. The poignant lyrics to *The Thief* come from a meeting Malcolm Mooney had with a Jewish friend, Zim, who kept telling him that he was taking the wrong path in life. This was a major contributory factor towards his subsequent departure.

Holger Czukay gets in touch with a friend in Switzerland, he asks him to build a sound-mixing desk with eight inputs for the group.

The group record a track called *Butterfly*, which is only released retrospectively in 1982, on the *Delay 1968* LP. Irmin Schmidt:

> "Most of the pieces that appeared on the *Delay 1968* LP were done just after or even before *Monster Movie*, but we didn't dare to put them on a record at that time. Instead of *Uphill* or *Butterfly* we chose other numbers, not so rough as the other stuff. Because we thought that *Father Cannot Yell* and even *Yoo Doo Right* seemed a little easier to understand. Now in 1982, it makes more sense to bring them out, with all these new groups who say they were influenced by Can. And we wanted to have "1968" in the title of this new album. It means a lot more for our French public than for the English or German ones, but we are definitely a '68 group." *(The significance of '68 refers to the student riots in Paris in May of 1968).*

They record a second version of *She Brings The Rain*.

Recording of the music for the film *Mädchen Mit Gewalt* by Roger Fritz. *Soul Desert* is the title song. Irmin Schmidt describes the song as, "Definitely the most desperate song that Malcolm sang, just the opposite of the beautiful love song *She Brings The Rain*."

At this time it is evident that Malcolm Mooney is really beginning to crack up and on the advice of a psychiatrist he returns to America. Michael Karoli:

> "He was happy musically, but not in his life. He was a black American and he didn't feel good in Germany. He had to go back to America."

1970

January/April Although the group were used to his unexpected absences (he sometimes forgot to turn up for a concert, or he disappeared right in the middle of it) Malcolm Mooney's departure leaves a deeply felt vacuum. The only recording released from this period is *Musette*, but the group still continue to work on material. They start working on the music for the film *Bottom* by Thomas Schamoni. The second version of *She Brings The Rain* (November '69) is used as the title song, its soft atmosphere contrasts with the hardness of the other pieces.

Around this time Abi Ofarim develops a strong interest in the group and becomes their manager, it is the beginning of a turbid and later, bitter relationship.

May

They play a four night engagement at the Munich discotheque *The Blowup*. One afternoon, Jaki Liebezeit and Holger Czukay are sitting outside a cafe when they hear a Japanese busker. The same evening, Kenji 'Damo' Suzuki, who is then 21 years old, gives his first concert as the vocalist of Can. Holger Czukay:

> "Yes, I was in this cafe with Jaki, and I saw Damo from far away, he was screaming and sort of adoring the sun. I said to Jaki, "Here comes our vocalist!" and Jaki said, "No, no, it can't be true", I said "Yes", and I went up to Damo and said, "Can you come tonight to the concert?" He accepted and he went right on stage. It was a furious concert, first Damo was singing very dramatically, it was very peaceful, he was very concentrated. And then like a samurai warrior he sprang up, he took the microphone in his hands and he screamed at the audience. The audience got so nervous, people began to hit each other, there was a fight and almost everybody left. At the end there were only some die-hard fans left, 30 Germans and 30 Americans, very enthusiastic, and the rest of the concert was just played for them. It was beautiful, a very good concert...
>
> Damo was a very different vocalist to Malcolm, but he was very concentrated and a highly fantastic vocalist. Fantastic in a way, with much fantasy."

June

Can compose the music for the film *Cream* by Leonidas Capitanos. Jaki Liebezeit plays flute on *Don't Turn The Light On, Leave Me Alone,* as well as providing some acrobatic drumming which gives an afro-cuban feeling to the piece.

July   The group work on the music for the film *Deep End* by Jerzy Skolimovsky. *Mother Sky* is one of the most intense pieces of rock music recorded by Can, and one of the few numbers that they agree has come off better on record than its limited number of live performances. The track is No 1 for weeks in Berlin, where it becomes a real discotheque favourite!

August   They record *Deadlock* and *Tango Whiskyman*, two title songs for the film *Deadlock* by Roland Klick.

September   A compilation LP of extracts from their last five film music projects is released entitled *The Can Soundtracks*.

October   One recording, *Blue Bag (Inside Paper)*, is an extract from one of the numerous long studio sessions. Here, Damo Suzuki improvises the lyrics about the blue garbage disposal bags, stuffed full of paper, that the group used to soundproof their studio.

November   Beginning of the *Tago Mago* sessions.

1971

February

End of the *Tago Mago* sessions. The project becomes a double-album, the second record containing more experimental pieces. The release of the album is delayed by Abi Ofarim, embittered by Hildegard Schmidt's succession to the management of the group. He takes out a court injunction to prevent the release of the album.

On *Aumgn*, Irmin Schmidt plays percussion and sings in a very concentrated way like in a magical ritual, and Jaki Liebezeit plays contra-bass. *Tago Mago* is the magic album of Can in every sense of the word. Tago Mago was the name of a magician, and 'Aumgn' is a magic formula by Aleister Crowley. Paul Alessandrini writes in the French monthly magazine *Rock & Folk*:

"This is a great record from a great group who oppose all the middle class concepts that affect rock music. After Amon Düül, discover Can, as the successor to the great American groups."

Many unreleased pieces exist from the *Tago Mago* sessions, like *E.F.S. No 27* which finally saw the light of day on the LP *Limited Edition*.

March

Hildegard Schmidt fully takes charge of the management of the group. *Turtles Have Short Legs* is released as a single in Germany with an edited version of *Hallelujah* on the other side.

April

Recording of *TV spot*. The Freak Out event, their second concert at *The Blowup* discotheque in Munich. Within the group there is some confusion over the exact details of the concert. Holger Czukay:

"The concert started quite normally, but later, the whole music changed completely. I smashed down the bass, I know, and then there was drumming or something like that. Then, after the interval, we came out and made a big noise by putting something on the organ keyboard. Then we sat down in front of the drums and started consuming cheese and wine."

Irmin Schmidt disagrees: "Well, I think it was coffee and cold chicken."

Holger Czukay: "I remember that Manfred Schmidt built up a table in front of the drums and served us lemonade and apfelstrudel with cream."

Irmin persists: "I know perfectly well, it was apple ketchup and weisburg."

Holger Czukay: "This concert I will never forget, not one second of it. How I was lying on the floor, playing my bass from that position."

Irmin Schmidt: "At the first *Blowup* gig we discovered Damo, and at this one we discovered David Niven — after the concert he said that it was one of the strangest shows he had ever seen in his life, he was really shocked."

Unfortunately, the group are not looking for a vocalist this time, and Mr Niven escapes.

June   Concert at the Aachen festival.

December   Can leave Schloss Norvenich and move their studio to an old cinema in Weilerswist, about 20 kilometres from Cologne.

Holger Czukay outside Schloss Norvenich in 1971.

The new studio is called Inner Space, in memory of the name of the very first incarnation of the group.

Their first work here is the recording of the music for *Das Messer*, a Francis Durbridge film for German TV. *Spoon* is issued as a single in Germany with *Shikaku Maru Ten* (A Japanese title meaning *A Square, Round Point*) on the B side, and the record becomes a number one hit, with sales topping 200,000 a few months later. It was always a favourite track of the group and was the name chosen by Hildegard Schmidt when she created Spoon Records in 1980.

1972

<u>February 3rd</u>   Free concert in the Cologne Sporthalle in front of 10,000 people. A juggler and a fire eater are on stage with Can. The event is filmed by Peter Przygodda for a 50 minute movie, *Can Free Concert*.

<u>March</u>   The Przygodda film includes new studio recordings, a new version of *Bring Me Coffee Or Tea* and two new pieces, *I'm Too Leise* and *LH 702 (Nairobi-München)*. The exact meaning of the title of this latter piece cannot be revealed for secret reasons. They also record *Vitamin C* for the Samuel Füller

thriller *A Dead Pigeon In The Beethovenstrasse*. It comes out as a single in Germany with *I'm So Green* on the B side. Right up until the last concerts in 1977, *Vitamin C* remains a stage favourite of the group, but *I'm So Green* has never been played live.

April/May

Can play their first tour of England, where United Artists released *Tago Mago* in a superb cover, different from the one used in Germany and France. The two LPs are slotted inside a single envelope folding cover, which opens up by detaching a tab that slots into the back cover. Duncan Fallowell comments on the sleeve notes to *Tago Mago*:

> "Can's music is intensely interwoven. Its surface is deceptively regular and beneath is an elaborate matrix of constantly shifting emphasis and cross-feeding, bulging in hypnotic spasms. Its effect is ectoplasmic and powerfully sexual."

They play an acclaimed concert in Colchester (Essex University, May 8th). The occasion is part of the university's rag week celebrations and Can perform in a cellar along with a slapstick act. Irmin Schmidt:

> "We didn't get any real contact with the audience at all. None of us really knew what was happening. The music got wilder and louder, it was really one of the most terrifying gigs we ever did."

But in spite of this loss of audience contact the gig took a most satisfying form. Beginning with a long mystical opening and development, the themes moving towards *Tago Mago*. At the end of the first half, the audience are too shocked to respond, and an eerie silence greets them. Holger Czukay:

> "They weren't able to do anything like clap, which wouldn't have fitted at all."

A bass theme from *Paperhouse* (the most lyrical piece in the concert) recurs in the second half, seemingly out of context. A stronger linking of the sections starts with a suggestion of *Hallelujah* long before its final apotheosis. The last hour is one long climax and sees the demise of the original audience, to be replaced by one that has heard on the grapevine that some extraordinary music being made. And at the end there is wild cheering and the realisation that the audience have witnessed a unique Can event. Duncan Fallowell writes, "There is so much intoxication in their music, so much catatonic madness... It's unbelievable."

June Sessions for *Ege Bamyasi (Okraschoten)*. Irmin Schmidt:

> "Just before the deadline, we needed one more piece. We improvised, made a few edits, and titled it *Soup*. It's one of the most spontaneous pieces we've ever done."

The name of the album came from a can that they found one day in a Turkish restaurant. Michael Karoli:

> "That was really by accident, and we couldn't call it anything else because the word "can" was already on it, it was the name of the company from Istanbul which manufactures these cans!"

The release of this album is also delayed by further court injunctions taken out by Abi Ofarim. The inside sleeve to the LP contains a typewriter generated quote from Shakespeare:

> *The man that hath no music in himself,*
> *Nor is not moved with concord of sweet sounds,*
> *Is fit for treasons, stratagems, and spoils,*
> *The motions of his spirit are dull as night,*
> *And his affections dark as Erebus;*
> *Let no such man be trusted.*
> *Mark the music!*

(In 1986, an English dance-technopop group with Pimlico Jones on guitar name themselves Ege Bam Yasi. They release a 12" called *Circumstance* (SUR T36) on the London-based label Survival Records).

August

Michael Karoli is taken seriously ill with a perforated ulcer, and Can are out of action until the new year.

Holger Czukay (bass guitar and piano) and Jaki Liebezeit (drums and percussion) help the German singer Alex to produce an LP of his Turkish-flavoured songs at the Inner Space.

November

Richard Williams writes in the *Melody Maker*:

"There's no doubt that Can are the most talented and consistent experimental rock group in Europe — and that includes Britain."

Michael Karoli recovers from serious illness in hospital.

1973

February

The group undertake their second English tour. The band uses a brand new J.B. Lansing eight track 2,000 watt P.A. which allows them to present a linear and clear sound. They play 20 concerts including two in London. Their first London concert at the Rainbow Theatre on February 18th is one of the most memorable gigs of the tour. Beginning in darkness, the audience is aware of some shadowy movements on stage, then a drum machine starts playing, gradually increasing in intensity. The audience joins in, clapping, but after 15 minutes becomes restless and eventually catcalls

"If you consider yourself in any sense involved with modern music, you cannot overlook them." *Spectator.*

develop.

The drumming fades and is replaced by Holger Czukay on transistor radio and Irmin Schmidt on keyboards. The lights gradually come on to reveal Damo Suzuki standing motionless at the front of the stage, his waist-length hair covering both the top-half of his body and the microphone. It is a full 30 minutes before the music is developed into a recognisable piece. A truly magical and mystical atmosphere is conjured.

During this period, Can concerts invariably begin to be sold out. The reputation of the group is growing, and *Ege Bamyasi* sells very well (about 10,000 copies in the first month in each country where it is released; Germany, France and England).

The music is often based on the *Ege Bamyasi* pieces *Vitamin C*, *One More Night*, *Spoon* and *Sing Swan Song*. They also play the first versions of *Full Moon On The Highway*. Irmin Schmidt plays steel-guitar for the first time. Irmin Schmidt:

"I was fascinated by this new instrument and I was playing it in a very personal way, not conventional at all, very rhythmically. At the end of the tour I liked it so much that I completely abandoned my keyboards, and Hildegard and Micky had to take the steel-guitar away from me!"

Spectator magazine comments in February:

"If you consider yourself in any sense involved with modern music, you cannot overlook them."

On March 16th Can play a live session at the BBC in London — the piece they play is called *Up The Bakerloo Line.*

March 22nd First concert in France, for the television broadcast *Pop 2.* Paul Alessandrini writes in *Rock & Folk':*

"One of the most amazing musical experiences any contemporary rock group can give you. The music is improvised, electro-acoustic melodies that range from wild to flamboyant, heart-rending to passionate. It's avant-garde in the sense that it makes use of every sound possibility, but at the same time it draws a physical response, willing you to dance..."

May 22nd Concert at the Paris Olympia.

June/July Summer break. Holger Czukay visits Thailand and other parts of the Far East to explore the music of this region. Damo Suzuki returns home to Japan for the first time in six years.

August Recording of the LP *Future Days.* The sessions begin with *Doko E*, a 45 minute piece (2' 28" will be extracted for *Limited Edition*) where Damo Suzuki sings in Japanese a beautiful text about the disappointing impressions he recently had of his native land, strongly supported by the metronomic drumming of Jaki Liebezeit. Then the group move into *Bel Air*, a collective improvisation which will be shortened to fill up the whole of side two of the album. (On the English pressing of the LP the track is named *Spare A Light*). Michael Karoli:

> "I had been holidaying in Portugal, and I used to go down to the beaches and absorb the sound of the sea and waves, just using my head as a kind of tape recorder. There, the beaches are often shaped in half-circles, with cliffs and sand around, and if you stand on one you can see the headlands of the others receding, less distinct in the mist each time, into the distance.
>
> When I went back to the studio I found that the echo machine that I was using with my guitar got this feeling of the cliff's outlines perfectly, with a strong chord, then a softer one, and so on. Then Irmin got the exact sound of the wind which was blowing in the house where I was staying, he even managed to get a tape-loop of a rare Indian bird recorded on location by some ornithologist, spending a full day in the Cologne recording archives to find it..."

Future Days went on to be proclaimed as the group's best LP by most of the rock press. Its royal blue cover is dominated by a large cabbalistic symbol in gold relief which is a stylised Greek letter psi, which stands for ESP, extra sensory perception. Ian MacDonald comments in the New Musical Express:

> "*Future Days* is sheer good music and is perfectly easy for anyone with a pair of ears attached to their heads, to get into and thoroughly enjoy...."

But the view that it was Can's best work to date was not

shared by Jaki Liebezeit:

"When we began it was great, everybody just had a few notes he could play so it stayed simple. But later our technical abilities increased, Holger could play very fast on his bass, Irmin could play a lot of technical things, and Micky could play very difficult things. It began with *Tago Mago*. I mean *Hallelujah* is monotonous, but not in the best way. And then it really went off with *Future Days*, I think, it became too symphonic."

<u>August 25th</u> The group play their last concert with Damo Suzuki, at the Edinburgh Festival. The band is recorded for a live album but on playing back the tapes they find that the guitar hasn't come out and so the project is abandoned.

<u>September</u> Damo Suzuki leaves Can.

Damo Suzuki photographed just before his decision to leave the group.

<u>October 23rd</u> Can play a free concert (concert-gratuit-zé-en direct) in the Grand Studio of RTL in Paris. Both the public and the group themselves seem to be confused by Damo Suzuki's absence.

<u>November</u> Can receive a letter from the ever-telepathic Malcolm Mooney from Harlem, suggesting a reunion. They send a return ticket for him to the New York Kennedy Airport but nobody comes...

The four remaining members of the group play their first full French tour including two long, crowded, legendary gigs, one at the Paris Olympia (November 25th) and the other at Nanterre University (December 10th) with them playing at least five encores at each concert.

December

Recording of the soundtrack for the Helma Sanders science fiction film *Gomorrha*. Its four descending semitones are often featured in various pieces at subsequent concerts as a basis for improvisations.

1974

January

German tour (Berlin, Hamburg, the Ruhr district) including one date at Mulhouse in France. The gig in Berlin is Can's longest ever concert, from 8.00 p.m. to 3.00 a.m. with an intermission.

February

Third English tour. Nick Kent writes in the New Musical Express about the Croydon concert (February 3rd):

"The music cannot be pin-pointed — it exists for itself and the audience seems bewildered, if occasionally invigorated by the more exotic passages... Only Can have motivated themselves out of the Krautrock zone to really merit superlatives as such."

The group play a session for the British TV programme *The Old Grey Whistle Test*. Their set is jokingly named *Set The Controls For The Art Of The Sun*. Can were often compared to Pink Floyd at the time. There is definitely a parallel between the history of the two groups in that their original singers both pushed themselves too far and went crazy, Malcolm Mooney temporarily, and Syd Barrett seemingly permanently.

Incidentally, at the end of '72 Can had declined the offer of supporting Pink Floyd for an English tour. This would have undoubtedly given them much more exposure, but they didn't want to shorten their set. They also refused to share the bill with anyone else except at festivals, believing that the

"Only Can have motivated themselves out of the Krautrock zone to really merit superlatives as such."
Nick Kent.

creation of a particular atmosphere was vital to the success of their music.

In February, Derek Jewell in *The Sunday Times* writes:

> "No band in the world illustrates the inadequacies of today's musical terminology more than Can."

March/April
Jaki Liebezeit, under the pseudonym Lee B. Zait, helps the singer Alex again on another LP entitled *That's The Deal*.

April
They return to France to play two concerts, at Poitiers (Festival Equinoxe) with Magma on the 13th, and in Nancy on the 16th.

May
The group record *E.F.S. No 36*, a dixieland jazz forgery on which Jaki Liebezeit plays trumpet.

June/August
The *Soon Over Babaluma* sessions begin. Michael Karoli plays violin and sings a text by Duncan Fallowell on *Dizzy Dizzy*. The track is one of the very first adaptations of reggae into rock music. Irmin Schmidt sings on *Come Sta, La Luna*, suggested by a friend to be a cha cha cha, but which turns out to be a hypnotic tango. Irmin Schmidt:

> "*Quantum Physics* is another of these last moment pieces, which concentrate all the creative process and the necessity of Can."

Steve Lake writes in Melody Maker, "Another great album from one of Europe's greatest bands!" The cover is one of Can's best. In England and Germany short versions of *Dizzy Dizzy/Splash* are released as a single.

Roger Greenaway writes in *Record Mirror*: "At no point do they try to imitate American or British rock styles, but produce a unique sound."

September
The group embark on their fourth tour of England, where

the retrospective album *Limited Edition*, compiled from their archives, is released simultaneously at a very cheap price (97 pence). Michael Karoli sings and plays the violin on stage from time to time. Michael Karoli:

"When the group began I was singing but I am not a singer, I am a guitar player, and doing the two at the same moment is not so easy. Regarding the violin, I very soon stopped playing it on stage because it never sounded good and always took my inspiration away."

In the following month of October, they play another session for the BBC, consisting of two pieces, *Return to BB City* and *Tape Kebab*.

1975

During a French tour 20,000 people see Can over the 11 concerts, the Bataclan in Paris is sold out twice, on the 17th and the 29th, where they play *Yoo Doo Right* as the encore. The live sound is very much improved with a new amplification system. Although Holger Czukay has an electric contrabass on stage he does not use it much. Holger Czukay:

> "I was trying to combine the technique of the contrabass and the electric system of a normal bass guitar."

Paul Alessandrini writes in 'Rock & Folk':

"Can is a magnificent machine; when they really get going they
are one of the most deafening groups on the rock music scene
today. Their burning desire is to go 'over the top'..."

In the Radio France archives, a mysterious Can tape exists
from January 30th, 1975, called *Zeste De Citron*, it lasts 4' 10",
is credited to Michael Karoli, and played by Can.

February/April Can go back into the studio, and take possession of a MCI 16
track recorder which will replace their old 2 track system.
With the new equipment they start working on the *Landed*
LP. *Red Hot Indians* has an afro-reggae feeling coming from
Jaki Liebezeit's drumming and saxophone riffs, later
completed during the mix by Olaf Kübler who was an old
friend of Jaki Liebezeit and became Amon Düül's producer.
The crowd noises were taped by Michael Karoli at Cologne
central station. *Full Moon On The Highway* has a hard rock
feel to it and was to be released in the USA in anticipation of
a tour which was later cancelled. *Hunters And Collectors* (a
single in Germany) and *Vernal Equinox* come from the same
session. Irmin Schmidt:

"*Unfinished* is a selection of a 45 minute session we called *The
Magic Day*, it was a very magical recording."

Michael Karoli:

"There was a whole evening when we had been talking about
things like recording and afterwards finding something on the
tape which nobody heard while it was being recorded, so we
decided to do the same thing, to put our equipment in and make
music by not doing anything. I've always known that you can
use the guitar strings as a kind of antenna for radio waves. There

Publicity photo for the *Landed* album recorded in1975.

we were in the studio and my guitar started playing something, and we got this kind of glockenspiel thing, indicative of Radio Moscow which we used in *Unfinished*. That wasn't magic, it was just inspired by it, we had so much magic in our heads. *Unfinished* is one of those pieces where we let the atmosphere of the studio impress itself on the tape, it's really a piece composed by the studio.

Later, I made this recording for *Red Hot Indians* in the Cologne Main Railway Station. I went around with my tape recorder in the hall and avoided coming close to anyone in order to get a continual buzz of conversation. And later when I played it back, on the last 20 seconds of the tape there was this very strange voice in German saying, "We are coming", with a South German accent and kind of distorted. I kept it, but we couldn't use it since it was too strong and didn't fit in anywhere. I can't explain how that came about because I kept well away from everyone."

Holger Czukay:

"*Landed* was very much controlled because it was done on a 16 track machine. We made a pre-mix before, discussed it, and so on. We were very much thinking about the drums because we had experienced some very bad circumstances during *Ege Bamyasi* and especially *Future Days* where the drums were too loud. That was due to our 2 track recording technique in those days. When we recorded *Bel Air* one of our roadies was controlling the mix, and afterwards we found that the drums were too loud. But the piece was so beautiful that we decided to leave it as it was.

During Malcolm Mooney's time, the balance was controlled by the whole group, not by myself, that's very important because everybody listened during the recording to the final mix as it went into the tape recorder, and was able to control himself. We became quite experienced at that, and the most important thing was that we didn't have too many playbacks. Later on, of course, we developed our recording technique. Can is a group where every record is developed differently."

May

Can sign with EMI's Electrola label in Germany and Virgin in England. Can was very much a natural signing for Virgin at this time as the label was concentrating on experimental music from England and Europe, including releases from Henry Cow, Robert Wyatt and Tangerine Dream amongst others.

The group leave for their fifth English tour and for the first time they play more or less structured concerts. The first set consists of *Chain Reaction* (a piece which enabled Michael Karoli to tune his guitar), *Bel Air*, *Dizzy Dizzy*, and the second set always beginning with *Pinch*. The way Can treated *Pinch* on stage, three years after the original version was recorded, was a good example of one of their favourite techniques — the generation of a mood through a very open rhythmic structure, and the maintenance of a tension, combined with melodic and rhythmic fluidity.

July

Can play two strong concerts at the Siegendorf Musik Forum in Austria on 9th and 13th. Can steal the show from the jazz and new musicians. During one of the concerts which was particularly brilliant, Michael Karoli asks the audience, "Can anyone bring us some wine?"

August 6th

Concert at the Arles Festival in France where they shared the bill with Kevin Ayers and Nico. For a lot of people it was one of the best concerts they played in France. Irmin Schmidt says that, "In the old amphitheatre it was wonderful, very relaxed..."

Hervé Picart writes in the French monthly magazine *Best:*

"One of the most staggering performances of their career; the group successfully sustained a fantastic climate of tension throughout — mind boggling!"

August 7th   Concert in Cannes, which like the one in Arles, remains a favourite of the group. Michael Karoli describes it as, "Just about the hottest we ever played. It was as though we had all suddenly achieved 'soul potential'."

August   Holger Czukay works in the studio with the Japanese female singer Michiko Nakao who overdubs vocals onto a few studio and live Can tapes. Holger Czukay:

"She made two spontaneous recordings on top of *Unfinished*. We might use them one day if we release another version of this piece."

Holger also records his own short piece (1' 50"), *Oh Lord Give Us More Money*. Irmin Schmidt:

"Holger had just seen a famous American preacher on TV and in the studio he did a funny imitation of him, using the ground tape of *Vernal Equinox*."

It was an early prelude to future successful solo experiments.

October 4th   Free concert in Paris (Théâtre de Chaillot) for the inaugural evening of the new France Musique radio programme. A wild gig with excerpts from *Landed*, including a powerful version of *Half Past One*. Very long extracts are broadcast. Claude Pupin, a French journalist, remembers the concert:

"How could I forget that evening? It was a dull day in late autumn. The '70s were still suffering from the abominations of the previous decade. Teenagers were having to rely on their imaginations to survive the decline of their old idols and the more ardent among them were quite prepared to cross the whole of Paris to pick up Can's latest release.

The German group had a foreign, exotic flavour that appealed to a 15 year old's fantasies and frustrations and this particular concert was no disappointment. Hysteria was already building up in the crowd waiting outside the Chaillot Theatre. There was fighting at the doors and some people were dropping like flies on a bad trip. And why? Can were giving their first real free concert so the kids were out in force, heads in a whirl, muscles twitching and mouths dry, high before the drugs even hit them.

First on the scene was Holger Czukay, striding over to the left of the stage as if he meant to stay there forever. Schmidt, Liebezeit and Karoli came on later, after Czukay had almost single-handedly stolen the show which the whole of Paris was waiting to see. With the four of them on stage it was 45 minutes of pure music, a communion of body and soul, metaphysically breaking the established rules..."

October

German tour. The best gigs are in Giessen (14th) and Saarbrucken (24th), where Holger Czukay takes his first steps as a singer during an unexpected version of *Oh Lord Give Us More Money.*

November

The group return to Britain for a short English tour. In Hatfield (21st) and in London, Drury Lane (23rd), Tim Hardin joins Can on stage to sing *The Man From Baltimore.* Irmin Schmidt:

"With Tim Hardin it was an opportunity, nothing was prepared. He was there, he liked what we were doing so he took his guitar and came to sing this piece with us. Some people always think that there is something behind these kinds of things, some mysterious plan of a record company! No, we just played together, that's all! Anyway, he was too much a 'songwriter' to become part of a group like Can. But he was incredible, he could always invent new songs."

December

Virgin records and Can agree on the release of a double album for the price of a single LP, including the old *Limited Edition* and a live record. In Cologne they listen to the tapes of the recent English concerts but are not satisfied with them and so prefer to compile a second record from their unreleased archives. Thus *Unlimited Edition* is released and again demonstrates the many different musical directions of the group.

1976

Can play a concert in Brussels. The morning of the concert they meet an Indonesian singer, Thaiaga Raj Raja Ratnam, who joins them on stage for one piece, just before the unexpected failure of the power supply which leaves Jaki Liebezeit alone on stage for a 10 minute drum solo. "I thought I was hallucinating when I saw the others leaving the stage...!" says Jaki Liebezeit

Raj only stays with Can for a few months. Holger Czukay:

"He came from Malaysia, knew how to listen and respect what

the other musicians did. With him, we only played two or three times on stage, but we recorded quite a lot of studio sessions."

Through Peter Gilmour, their live sound-mix man who also wrote the lyrics on *Landed*, *Flow Motion* and *Saw Delight*, Can meet the English singer Michael Cousins. Irmin Schmidt:

"At this time we were really looking for a new vocalist and when we had the offer we took the risk and took him on stage with us, without knowing what he would do exactly."

After a gig in Lille the day before, this new format of Can plays the Salle Wagram in Paris on March 19th. The audience attempts to spit at Cousins and to drown him out by shouting, and at times the noise rivals Can's 2,500 watts of sound. Irmin Schmidt:

"I liked the reaction of the public very much, they really showed their feeling, without being polite at all. When Michael Cousins was singing they shouted, and when we were only playing instrumentally they loved it. It was a very strange gig, very dislocated."

Holger Czukay:

"This singer had a sort of heavy rock style, and Can is sometimes a heavy rock group, but only sometimes..."

Michael Karoli:

"In our music the singer must be soft, and he was not like this. His nickname was Magic Michael! Yes, he was very magical, in a way, like Frank Sinatra!"

The group undertake a German tour with Michael Cousins, but he leaves shortly after. In the mid-80s he was last reported to be working as a bus driver in London.

Michael Rother asks Jaki Liebezeit to play the drums for his *Flammende Herzen* LP. He subsequently becomes Rother's regular drummer and appears on the following albums; *Flammende Herzen* (Sky, 1977), *Sterntaler* (Sky, 1978), *Katzenmusik* (Sky, 1979) and *Fernwärme* (Polydor, 1982).

The group begin sessions for the *Flow Motion* LP. *I Want More* will enter the charts in England and will be Can's first and only British hit single. Irmin Schmidt sings on *Babylonian Pearl*.

However, Jaki Liebezeit was once again expressing reservations about the more technical approach the group were taking:

> "We have too much technical ability at the moment. We have too many things that distract us. It is like if you are a good speaker you may use too many words, and if somebody says to you, "Tell me the way to so and so", you talk for half an hour and still they can't find the place. Then somebody else comes along and makes a gesture and they find it immediately. Too many thoughts distract you from the simplicity."

The group record a version of the Christmas carol *Silent Night* for a single. Irmin Schmidt:

> "It didn't work on a commercial level, but musically we liked it a lot. In Germany the radio stations did not play it at all, because for them a reggae-rock version of *Silent Night* was really blasphemy!"

They record a live session for a television broadcast in London. In another studio Rosko Gee (a former member of Traffic) is rehearsing and he becomes friends with Holger

Czukay:

"Rosko had seen us in concert once in London and he loved us. I asked him to come to Cologne and he began to play bass guitar with Can, while I became involved with other things... Yes, I brought Rosko into the group. That's destiny, and destiny is never strange."

Irmin Schmidt:

"At this time Holger was not happy in the group, and it was him that introduced Rosko to us. When Rosko came to Cologne and began to play with us, we all liked what he did, and Holger tried other personal instruments. There is a time when things must change."

December 4th Concert at the London New Victoria Theatre. The set includes a fabulous version of *Pinch*. Rosko Gee plays bass while Holger Czukay concentrates on using tapes, a short-wave radio and a telephone. Holger Czukay:

"When I began to play the radio with Can, I thought we had found not one singer but thousands! It reminded me of my enthusiasm when I had my first radio when I was 14! With the radio, my idea with Can was to use a short-wave transmitter, to be able to broadcast the concerts of the group. I wanted to become the sort of disc jockey of Can — the people would have heard what I was saying and what I was broadcasting, and maybe some amateur would have replied from any place in the world, his message coming on stage with the band. The telephone was more a sort of joke but I had a secret dream — I wanted to be able to call up anyone during a concert, and inject their voice into the music..."

1977

January

The group start sessions for *Saw Delight*, which turns out to be their prophetic "world music" album. The opening piece, *Don't Say No*, is a sort of 'disco' remake of *Moonshake*. *Sunshine Day And Night* is influenced by 'high life music' which Michael Karoli discovered during a long visit to Kenya. *Animal Waves* is based on a Rumanian gypsy tune. In Germany, *Don't Say No* is released as a single, with *Return* on the B side, an out-take from *Animal Waves*. The percussionist Reebop Kwaku Baah (like Gee also ex-Traffic) is involved in the sessions. Irmin Schmidt:

Rosko Gee
who replaced
Holger Czukay
as the group's
bass player.

"Nothing was prepared at all. Rosko and Reebop knew each other, and Rosko is always happy when Reebop is around. When we began *Saw Delight*, Reebop played percussion, and he began to sing as well, in a very spontaneous way. He really stimulated the other musicians and for me he was an extraordinary influence, one of the strongest of my musical life. It was completely magic, a bit like the old days."

March

The group play their seventh English tour. At the London Sound Circus on March 27th, Reebop plays on stage with Can for the first time. The conflicts grow between Holger Czukay and the other musicians. Holger Czukay:

"Yes, there were problems, mainly with the radio. It's a pity, because the relationship between the musician and the radio is really magical. But you have to forget your ego as a musician, it is not easy. And with Can it didn't work."

Irmin Schmidt:

"I have very mixed feelings from this period. It was obvious that there were a lot of problems. Some parts were really nice, but basically Holger's radio stuff would have blended much more with the group as we were before, but not with Rosko and Reebop. It wasn't fitting together, more because of the gesture toward rock music than because of the music itself.

The biggest contrast was between Reebop and Rosko on one side, and Holger on the other side. In fact, Holger started to develop what he did later on his own. But everybody felt that something was deeply changing in the group. And when you are involved in creation, these changes are sometimes very painful."

April 21st

Can play a concert in Cologne. Manni Löhe, their old friend from the Schloss Norvenich days, attends the gig and climbs on stage to dance. He will die a few months later, in January 1978. Their typical repertoire from this period includes pieces from *Saw Delight* (except *Fly By Night*), *I Want More*, *Flow Motion*, sometimes *Cascade Waltz*, plus various unreleased numbers and old pieces like *Vitamin C* and *Dizzy Dizzy*. Irmin Schmidt:

"We played them because there was still a potential in them. Once we couldn't really recreate something new with an old piece, we dropped it immediately from our repertoire."

May 2nd

The group play another concert in Paris, this time at the Théâtre Le Palace. Another typical repertoire from this period is, *Flow Motion, Don't Say No, Animal Waves, Dizzy*

Dizzy, I Want More, Sunshine Day And Night. Holger Czukay wears a blue suit studded with bright stars and seems more and more isolated from the rest of the group.

May 20th

In Geneva they play their last concert with Holger Czukay. He goes back to Germany and then flies to Hong Kong for a holiday. The indication that there would continue to be collaborations between Holger and the other members of Can in the future is hinted at by Michael Karoli:

> "Holger cannot really leave, it's impossible. He left a formation, but he didn't leave Can."

Irmin Schmidt:

> "Hildegard made it possible for Holger to recover from the pain of leaving the group, and helped him to create new things. All the personal difficulties didn't lead to a catastrophe, she made it work without any animosity."

End of May

Can play their last gigs before disbanding, in Spain (Madrid and Barcelona) and in Portugal (Lisbon and Porto). The very last concert in Lisbon is a great success, and Can play in front of 10,000 people. There are riots in the audience.

October

Sessions begin for the *Out Of Reach* LP, which has a title which says it all. Subsequently, it is an album which will disappoint everybody, not least the musicians themselves. Irmin Schmidt:

> "*Out Of Reach* is certainly representative of Can at this time, but it is hard for me to identify with it. For example, I do not feel magic in it. Some people liked it. Not me."

Michael Karoli echoes the same sentiments:

"Everybody felt that something was deeply changing in the group. And when you are involved in creation, these changes are sometimes very painful."
Irmin Schmidt

"I am very disappointed, it is not a good record. It comes obviously from Rosko, who composed two numbers under his own name, something we had never seen before in Can. You know, Can function as a geometry of people — it may be a triangle, a rectangle, or a quincunx figure, but there is never someone out of it who is leading the others, never."

Can material had always been sensitive to the exterior environment and the circumstances under which they were recorded. *Ege Bamyasi,* maybe their bleakest LP was recorded during a rainy summer and at the beginning of Michael Karoli's illness, while *Future Days* and *Soon Over Babaluma* were conceived in radiant summers, which one can feel in the music. However, with *Out Of Reach*, their least successful LP, it is not surprising that it cruelly reflects a period of crisis and of infertility.

December

They record the single *Can Can/Can Be*, based on a famous theme by Offenbach, which is released in Germany in early '78 to celebrate Can's tenth birthday, Michael Karoli plays guitar and bass. Incidentally, Offenbach founded the Cologne opera, and like Can, lived in Cologne. Irmin Schmidt describes the record as, "A sort of joke." but he also points out:

"Offenbach was quite revolutionary, and the can-can was a very vulgar dance, almost underground. Now, that is forgotten because it belongs to the classical music world... So, as a kind of hommage we made our version vulgar as well, almost punk!"

1978

February   They begin sessions for the LP *Can*, which is received more favourably when it is released. The group themselves also seem to be happier with the record. Michael Karoli:

> "I like it a lot, the music is much more balanced between all the members. All emotional gates are open again..."

Irmin Schmidt:

> "It is a good album. For example, *Safe* is a real Can piece — when I mixed the LP with Michael, we reduced the parts of

115

Reebop Kwaku
Baah.

influence of Rosko and Reebop, it turned out that we could musically integrate them. On *A Spectacle*, Holger helped us a lot and his editing was really a part of the composing. At this moment, Holger was a member of Can again."

A Spectacle is used with a different mix (in mono) as the theme tune for the German TV cultural programme *Aspekte*. Irmin Schmidt also commented at this time:

"There are no new directions. The main thing is that there is no old direction any more, which is quite good because people must get rid of old things to create new ones."

Autumn

Release of *Cannibalism* in England, a double-album compiled by Duncan Fallowell. The cover text is written by Pete Shelley who is at that time the leader and guitarist with The Buzzcocks. Irmin Schmidt:

"It's quite a good selection, we had to edit some of the longer pieces like *Soup* or *Mother Sky*, but we kept the full version of *Yoo Doo Right* - it was our first record and it means so many things for us. Also *Yoo Doo Right* represents for a lot of people the whole sense of Can's music. So this piece couldn't be edited, you know."

End of 1978

Can decide to suspend their activities as a group for an indefinite period. However, it is clear that although not operating under the collective name Can, individual members of the group would be collaborating in the near

Can decide to suspend their activities as a group for an indefinite period.

117

future. Michael Karoli:

"Of course it is possible that Can will play together again, but never as a working group doing nothing else. Can may exist only as a recording unit, with maybe a few gigs from time to time."

Rosko Gee leaves Germany, Reebop joins the Jimmy Cliff community (he will later move to Sweden and will die there at his home in Stockholm after suffering a brain haemorrhage in January '83). Jaki Liebezeit plays with various groups in Cologne before founding Phantom Band, Michael Karoli moves to France, and Irmin Schmidt and Holger Czukay involve themselves in their respective solo projects.

MALCOLM **M**OONEY

MALCOLM MOONEY WAS BORN IN YONKERS, NEW YORK, into a community near the Hudson River where he went to the local state school. As a child he always wanted to play music. His father, who was from North Carolina and was known in his home town as a musician, was a piano player. His father also always used to play the piano in the house that the family lived in Yonkers, having bought a piano for Malcolm's sister.

However, the first instrument that the young Mooney tried was an accordion, but it was an instrument he found difficult to play as he kept getting confused with the sharp and flat

Michael Karoli
and Malcolm
Mooney
rehearsing in
1969.

buttons on the left side of the accordion.

The Mooney household was always full of music, his father was always playing records and they used to listen to the radio — especially the jazz stations that came on at night. His first introduction to rock 'n' roll was in 1956 through a record by Frankie Lymon called *Why Do Fools Fall In Love*, it was a song that struck a chord with him as he was just entering puberty and had fallen in love with a girl from around the corner and this song seemed very appropriate. Living on a hill, he used to look out the window at this girl, and make up a song to her.

In the fourth grade he was given a clarinet, and he would practice hard for days, especially before the graduation concert by the school orchestra. However, during the concert he hit a high note which was completely out of tune and the music master looked at him and sternly pointed him out in front of the audience. He never played clarinet again. He stayed in state school up until the tenth grade, where he used to play a lot of sport, especially baseball, basketball, and running. Due to his sporting ability he was offered a scholarship to a private boarding school where instead of having thirty pupils in the classroom there were only five or six. In turn the school asked everyone to play three sports a year.

He was not involved with music much at this time apart from when he used to return home from boarding school and he and five friends would sit around singing in a church basement, pretending that they were an old rock 'n' roll group and trying to make up songs. Mooney always wanted to be the lead singer, but he thought his friend Bobby Simmonds, who now has a group in California, had a better voice and he thought he could never be the lead singer while Bobby was in the group. However, being brought up a protestant he had other opportunities to sing as he was also a member of the church choir.

Malcolm Mooney rehearsing with Can at Norvenich, September 1968.

He then started to go to a lot of jazz clubs and hear people like John Coltrane and Charlie Mingus and subsequently his musical orientation became a compilation of jazz and rock 'n' roll. He used to like the 'doo wah' groups as they were called. He was impressed by their fantastic harmonies, even

though sometimes they were off key just a little bit. Later on his interest in harmony groups led to him listening to The O'Jays and The Temptations and the early Motown groups.

As well as jazz and soul, he was also interested in rock 'n' roll which had stemmed from the time Elvis Presley came on the scene. However, Mooney's interest in Elvis came about very much through the back door, after hearing old blues singers like Muddy Waters, Howlin' Wolf, Lightening Hopkins and Robert Johnson.

At this time he was still in college, but he had played some music in Boston with some jazz-orienatated musicians — but he wasn't singing, he played a broken down piano by just plucking the strings. It was at this time that he was given his first saxophone, and he started practising with a friend of his called Chuck Davis, an alto player who had lived in Europe for ten or twelve years. Davis told him that he would never be that great a sax player, but Mooney continued to have ambitions as a saxophonist as well as a singer.

Malcolm Mooney left for Europe on April 27th, 1968, flying by way of Iceland and landing in Luxemburg. He hitchhiked a while with a friend Joshua Zim, who is no longer alive, but whose spirit Mooney considers is still very much out there somewhere. Their first stop was Paris, having arrived just after the student riots, they noticed that the police were carrying machine guns and the whole city looked like everyone was on alert. In Paris he stayed with a composer friend Serge Tcherepnin who Mooney had first met at New York University where Tcherepnin was involved with an experimental programme with about ten artists.

In Paris, Tcherepnin also introduced Mooney to another composer, Emmanuel Nunez, who was writing a composition at that time for 800 million Chinese to be sung at one time in unison. Although Nunez didn't speak much

English, Mooney enjoyed meeting him and said that they communicated musically.

After leaving Paris, Mooney and Zim travelled South, with the idea of eventually heading for India. They went to Avignon, where they met a man called Joe Palluca, who was a boxer at the time, and he took them to a club, and Mooney ended up playing saxophone while Palluca played the piano. It was difficult to know whether the music pleased the audience, but at the end of the concert, Joe Palluca got out his hat and passed it through the audience. He was so big that it was difficult for them to say no. So they got paid.

Then he went to Spain, Ibiza, and back through Algeciras after being refused entry to Spanish Morrocco. Then eventually they travelled north again up to Salzburg, and picked up the train from Salzburg to Istanbul. They stayed in Istanbul until they met this crazy guy who drove them to Tehran, then catching a bus to Mashhad, a boat to Karachi, and finally on to Bombay. They then turned back toward Europe, ending up first Munich and then back to Paris. In Paris he met Hildegard Schmidt for the first time, and Hildegard told him about Irmin starting a music group and having a studio in Cologne. There was a misunderstanding and Mooney thought they were talking about a studio for painting, so when he arrived in Cologne with just 80 pfennig in his pocket, he was surprised to find a music studio. First he phoned Irmin Schmidt's house and there was no answer. So he walked around looking for the house, and then he came upon a woman walking her dog, so he asked her if she knew Irmin Schmidt, and by pure coincidence she turned out to be Irmin Schmidt's sister. So she took him to Irmin's house, and that was how he first met the group.

Malcolm Mooney arrived in Cologne at a time when Can was at its birth, but a good relationship soon developed

Malcolm Mooney recording with Can after an absence of 17 years.

between the musicians. So, Irmin asked Mooney if he could sing, and he told Schmidt that he had sung with the church choir, so they started practising in Norvenich with Mooney as the singer. Malcolm Mooney recalls the early days with the group:

"We practised a lot. The first time I remember playing was in front of the people from the consulate at the Schloss Norvenich. The studio sessions were quite mad, but a good type of madness, there were a lot of things that I had never heard before. They all knew each other, so I was the new man on the block. But, it just started to gel for some reason or another. Irmin says that the band has the tendency to drive all its singers crazy. It was a very rigorous time we had together, because not many groups rely on that sort of spontaneity - not in the rock business, anyway.

I had never worked so hard as I did in Schloss Norvenich, we would play from 1 p.m. in the afternoon through to 1 a.m. at night straight through with a few breaks to go to the loo or get something to eat. I remember *Yoo Doo Right*, going on for hours, I left with Micky and climbed out of the studio window, went to a restaurant, ate, and when we came back they were still playing the song, so we went right back into it, it was like a never-ending piece. It was quite an event."

When Mooney first started singing he didn't know how to deal with an audience until the group played the music for the play *Prometheus* at the Schauspielhaus in Zurich in 1969, when there was a lot of controversy about the group's performances. Malcolm Mooney:

"I remember picking a woman out of the audience to sing to, I didn't have any idea what Prometheus was all about, I mean when I wrote the lyrics, I had no idea about his liver being eaten by a raven. Some of my lyrics were about flying to the moon, or something!"

Mooney often used to improvise the lyrics to the pieces, but there was usually a basic structure or idea worked out beforehand. Malcolm Mooney:

"*Yoo Doo Right* was actually a take off of a letter I got from my girlfriend at the time, and in it she wrote "you do right", and that became a lyric. There were a number of pieces I wrote down, mostly from the top of my head — I'm a dreamer."

Mooney only stayed as the singer with Can for fourteen months, but his influence on the other members was still very strong. There were times when his strong personality seemed to be almost leading the band — he was also

Self Portrait 1979 - Malcolm Mooney. Acrylic on paper.

responsible for naming them. However, at the end of 1969, he decided to leave the group after what he described as "Too much... Too soon". Also, in Zurich, Mooney had heard the other four members rehearsing by themselves with no vocals, and it sounded so great that the idea occurred to him to leave. Malcolm Mooney:

> "I had become so attached to Can, my heart kept saying stay, my mind kept saying go. So, I became ill... For the first few years, I was quite angry at myself, for having the difficulty I was having. Up until the June of '70 I was interested in going back to the group immediately, but I was having a great deal of emotional problems, so I couldn't leave New York. There was lot of unfinished business in America — I hadn't seen my family in two years."

After deciding to stay in the States, Mooney took a number of different jobs. But he involved himself primarily with art, working in New York for the Museum of Modern Art, and then the Metropolitan Museum. He also worked as a printer for a while, but nothing was long term. In 1977 his father passed away and it changed his perspective a great deal — Mooney and his father were planning on starting a printing business together and when he died the idea was shelved.

In 1980 he had an exhibition in the Hudson River Museum, where he re-met a woman that he had known when he was a college student, but who lived in California. In December '81 he received a $500 telephone bill, so he worked out it would probably be cheaper to go out to California than make all these phonecalls. He didn't return to New York until December '87. During his time in California he worked in Los Angeles at various galleries and went back to University to get his masters degree in fine art.

Since leaving Can, Mooney has not been in any other

groups — his only other musical performance being when he sang with a woman playing the piano at a happening in New York at the artist Fred Brown's studio. He invented a song on the spot for the occasion which was called the *Paternity Suit Blues*, "I don't know why, but that suggested itself to me as the good name for a song." He also played for a while with a trumpet player called Charlie Magee.

But he still listened to a lot of music and in 1983 he re-met Chuck Davis, who used to teach him sax, and they used to hang out at the bistro, and he still felt an urge to make music. He says that his interests are music, theatre, painting and sculpture and he still wants to continue those. For instance, he has continued to keep abreast of current music trends. Malcolm Mooney:

"I know the manager of the Fat Boys, and he has introduced me to rap music and it is definitely a new sound, I'm not too sure I want to hear it forever, but it's a stepping stone. They have an inventiveness about them, the only thing that I don't appreciate about it is the fact that its only singing, there's no instrumentation and when they go on the road it's not a group."

Since January 1988 he has lived in New York where he teaches children from second, third and fourth grade who are below their reading level. He is involved in a programme which attempts to help them to read better through involving the children with the arts.

In 1986, after nearly 17 years absence from Can, he rejoined the other four founder members and they started recording new material. However, Mooney had never totally discounted recording with the group again. When asked about a reunion in an interview with Archie Patterson in the American *Eurock* magazine in 1983:

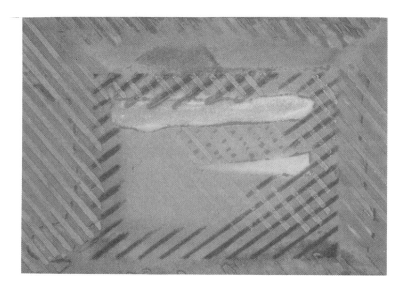

Papa Fauv
Malcolm
Mooney, 1987
Acrylic on
paper.

"I'd love to have a chance! As for doing anything musically again, we'll have to wait and see."

The reunion actually came about after Mooney had been talking to Hildegard Schmidt on the phone, he had also hinted at the possibility of a reunion in a letter to her. Coincidentally, around the same time the group were having the same thoughts about a reunion record, so it seemed that the idea was almost telepathic. Malcolm Mooney:

"I have always wanted to come back to Can, but I never knew when I could feel comfortable in myself. I still listened to their music, stuff like *Soon Over Babaluma* and *Unlimited Edition*, but I found what I was interested in for the most part was extending my range of other information. I knew Can, but I wanted to see if there was more I could use in my material that could be helpful to someone.

So, when the telepathy worked and we were planning to do another record, I had a lot of material written from the '70s and I would get into these songs like *Drugs and Bugs* and *Below This Level*, lyrics which were written in 1975. I had kept them all in a book. And then in 1986, Jaki presented me with some books of material that I had wrote but left behind in 1968/9, so material also came from those books for this new album."

Mooney hadn't played with Can for 17 years, but when Jaki and Irmin came and picked him up from the airport at Nice, he went straight out to the studio, had some breakfast and then went in and played. At that point he realised there was something good still happening. Malcolm Mooney:

"The chemistry to me was still working. It is an interesting phenomena. I'd like to be an egotist and say that we're great. I think in the way that we play, each individual has to say that —

it gives you strength and confidence and that is a big key."

Whether the reunion is a temporary one, or constitutes something more permanent remains to be seen. Malcolm Mooney:

"Like the tune says, "In the distance lies the future." All of us have different situations, so it would have to be joint decision to do that.

DAMO **S**UZUKI

Kᴇɴᴊɪ 'ᴅᴀᴍᴏ' sᴜᴢᴜᴋɪ ʙᴇᴄᴀᴍᴇ ᴀ ʙᴇᴀᴛɴɪᴋ ɪɴ ᴊᴀᴘᴀɴ ɪɴ 1966 and wishing to take part in the international hippy movement, he left Japan in the same year. He had heard a lot of music through the American military which had influenced him, and had gained a connection with some of the underground groups from California. From 1968 he started busking around Europe with a broken guitar. He was the epitome of the true busker, often he played with just four strings since he could not afford the new ones. He travelled mainly in Scandinavia, Germany and France. Damo Suzuki:

Damo Suzuki became Can's singer after they discovered him busking outside a Munich café.

"I could play just three chords on my guitar, and I didn't have any real music in my head, I was playing the music of the people, real improvisation."

The name Damo came from a comic strip character for whom everything was always going wrong. This very much typified his character at that time. So, suddenly he acquired the name and became Damo:

"This is OK, but Jaki sometimes sees sinister connotations in the name, such as *Dangerous Active Mode Organisation.*"

He first met Can when he was in Munich busking at a popular meeting place for hippies. He was also involved with the musical *Hair* at the time, but was becoming fed up with the routine of playing the same kind of music all the time. He didn't practice anything before going on stage with Can, his first concert with the group was totally spontaneous — as a street musician he had been used to improvising. Before playing the guitar, he had also played saxophone and clarinet but within Can he concentrated on vocals, developing his very special kind of vocal improvisation. Damo Suzuki:

"I can't sing, so I used the voice as an instrument. I'm not so much interested in anything in particular, that's why I'm singing about nothing. I improvise melody and texture too, so I

Damo Suzuki in concert.

don't concentrate on one thing. Sometimes it sounds like English, French or German, but really it is the language of the Stone Age."

It was Damo's ability to use his voice as another instrument that influenced some of the New Wave bands in the late '70s who cited Can as an influence. Mark E. Smith founder of The Fall:

"A big inspiring thing was early Can stuff, when they had Damo Suzuki. He wasn't even singing lyrics, in fact, he didn't even know what he was singing, the Japanese guy, he was learning English, and he was just saying words. And that's what inspired me." (Quote from *Tape Delay* by Charles Neal).

On The Fall's 1985 album *This Nation's Saving Grace* there appears a track called *I Am Damo Suzuki*, written by Mark E. Smith, Brix Smith and Karl Burns. Also, in February 1988, Smith told the *New Musical Express* that they wanted to do something extreme to their version of The Kinks' *Victoria*, "sort've almost like early Can". Even more recently in *Sounds*, Mark Smith described how he had met Damo Suzuki in Germany and how Damo had given him a tape of some new material which he had liked.

Damo's voice may sometimes be compared to the vocal style of his compatriot Yoko Ono in the harder pieces by the Plastic Ono Band, recorded in the early '70s around the same period. In 1978 Kenneth Ansell in *Impetus* wrote:

"Whereas Damo's real power seems to be in his free form scat singing and his destruction of the ability to understand the literal meaning of words."

Damo recalls much of the music he made with Can:

"The group had no actual pieces composed before recording the albums — we just played. The first take of *Mushroom* was just Holger, Jaki, and me, with some guitarist who played violin. We found it very good and played it again — it was OK. With *Sing Swan Song* I played it alone, then the others did some overdubs on the melody. *Hallelujah* was Jaki and Holger on the first take, then I did a vocal over it, then Michael and Irmin added parts. My vocals were totally improvised, I didn't care, I didn't take any care over that, the words have nothing to do with the music.

Full Moon On The Highway was maybe too easy, just two chords, I had composed it during my days as a street musician, that was my piece and my name should have been on the credits when the others released it later on their *Landed* album. *I'm So Green* was quite hard, but it is a really nice piece, everything for me is really perfect as improvised music there. *Don't Turn The Light On, Leave Me Alone* I don't like too much, I was totally confused, it was my first take with Can, and at that time I used to listen to some really heavy music like Grand Funk and Deep Purple and I couldn't get into the piece.

To my taste Can wasn't a good studio group, we played much better live. Can did *Shikaku Maruten* live, together with *One More Night*. *Shikaku Maruten* came about because I had trouble counting the 7/8 beat, and this was an easier way."

In September 1973 Damo Suzuki married a German girl whose parents were Jehovah's Witnesses. He became converted himself and decided to leave Can. Damo Suzuki:

"Also, I didn't like to become some kind of pop star and become involved in show business. Actually I was quite young, just 23, and I felt I had much more possibility for learning. It was really boring. With *Future Days* I think it was really musically very good, but it was really distant music for me. It was more

"I don't need many material things, I need time to play and laugh and excite."

classical and more elemental than at the beginning, not so much of a freak out. I couldn't live with that thing much more because I lived with much more far out music. Can became like Hollywood music, then some kind of folk music, then African music. Quite distant for me. I didn't like to make music after those things. In fact, I cannot say that my wife had any effect on my decision to leave the group."

After leaving Can, Damo Suzuki settled in Dusseldorf with his wife and two children — he also began working for a big Japanese company. However, he still continued to keep in touch with Can, especially with Holger Czukay. At the end of the '70s Hildegard Schmidt commented:

"He comes to visit the studio, and sometimes when he receives a cheque for his royalties with Can, he takes his guitar and tells his wife, "You see, I'm still making money with them!"

In 1978-1979 he tried to work with Holger Czukay and Jaki

Liebezeit again, but it didn't work. Damo Suzuki:

"It was too composed. We played together because we liked each other, but musically nothing was really good."

In 1984, Damo Suzuki went back to the professional music circuit again and became the singer of the German band Dunkelziffer, an already established group. He made two albums with them. Damo Suzuki:

"Dunkelziffer comprised Stefan Kreuten (drums), Reiner (percussion), Oleg (percussion), Wolfgang (sax), Dieke (bass guitar), Dominik von Senger (guitar), Mattias Keus (keyboards), Jumpy Szall (keyboards) and me. I left the group in March 1987 because there were too many melody instruments in the group. We did about 50 live gigs together, as well as some TV spots."

In 1986 Damo and his wife divorced after a 13 year

The Damo
Suzuki Band -
Dominik von
Senger, Damo
Suzuki, Jaki
Liebezeit,
Mattias Keus.

marriage. He then formed the Damo Suzuki Band, with Dominik von Senger from Dunkelziffer (guitar), Mattias Keus (keyboards), and Jaki Liebezeit. The band's first sessions took place in May 1987. Damo Suzuki:

"We are only a live group, we play spontaneous music. We did about 40 concerts in 1988, but we don't want to make records. In fact, we'd like to do only one or two gigs a month — doing any more we would not be so good because everything we play is new, we don't like to play the same thing again. We just play music for today, we don't practice anything, we just go on stage and play music with no concepts before the music starts. Can had so much more material because of their records, we have no records so no preconceptions of this sort. But sometimes we play *Hallelujah*, sometimes *Spoon* as well, because you must remember that out of the four people, two of them are from Can... Sometimes Jaki plays something like *Spoon* and I take it up, it just happens...

One night in Berlin one piece was 20 minutes long and Dominic played only one note, I like those kind of things — the audience are always wondering what is going to happen. We don't have a bass guitar in the group because it is disturbing to Jaki. It is nicer this way, since Jaki plays really good drums, I also think that one person for the rhythm section is enough."

Today, Damo Suzuki's style of vocalising within the Damo Suzuki Band is still essentially the one he developed with Can, but the music shows a strong element of extended improvisation, to a greater extent than was the case with the other groups with which Jaki Liebezeit was connected (Phantom Band etc). There is no doubt that today, Damo Suzuki is one of the guardians of the Can spirit.

Apart from the Damo Suzuki Band, he still works for a Japanese electronics company. "It is a very good job", explains Jaki Liebezeit, "He can go and do a concert whenever he wants." Much of this dual role is born out of the fact that he doesn't think that music is necessarily the best thing in life. Damo Suzuki:

"I don't need very much success, I'm enjoying my life in my own style, I don't need many material things, I need time to play and laugh and excite."

He also has a group in Dusseldorf with Thomas Dinger (ex-La Düsseldorf) and Niels Christianson. The band is called 1a Düsseldorf. "We are a studio group", explains Damo, "We have done a couple of tracks that we should mix."

The following texts give some idea of his incredible gift for word manipulation. However, these lyrics were transcribed by Duncan Fallowell and he has commented that they only approximate to the incomprehensible sounds made by Damo on the records. Duncan Fallowell:

"Damo just used to make any sound that came into his head — but Can needed an actual text, by law, for publishing the songs in certain countries, so I went through all the Damo tracks and wrote them down. In fact, I'd say that the lyrics as they are written down have little to do with Damo — although I claim no great literary merit for them."

PINCH

Don't do that when you're all alone
I couldn't pay you to take you home
I'm gonna press your ears on the light
And later I'll leave the way you go
Hey, that cow is moaning alone
Are you sure that I can call me — bleat!
Wanted to try a proposal road
Nobody comes when you won't be blowed
Are you cool now, now they say
Want you alone, how are you going home
Which one is you, you liar
Want your head alone
Want your time, give you help, you're so lonely
Hey, you know that I hypnotise.
Hey, did you want that to really bomb
No I do not, no, no, hey, hey
Nobody I knew had that tone
Nobody I knew sounded so proud
You should have known, you always should
Finish your tea
You take a dollar and you're gonna blow
You should have said it — I'm feeling unwell
Nobody saw, I keep to your ways
The heat is small in your peculiar life
I said you babe
You're moaning alone
I only want a cigarette — to make me cry and moan
You just admit it — you're all alone
Nobody's taking us off the 'phone
You're just alone and I've got you
Alone at night and when you talk
I want you alone
You piss off and it looks bad
You're lying alone and it isn't the boy either
Keep that talk empty, like you
Eyes stare — pinch...

VITAMIN C

Her daddy's got a big aeroplane
He mummy holds all the family cash
A beautiful rose is standing in the corner
She is living in or out of tune

Hey you, you're losing, you're losing,
You're losing, you're losing your Vitamin C

Giant press machine one her body
She is stepping on a quicksand
A beautiful rose standing in the corner
She is living in or out of tune

Hey you, you're losing, you're losing,
You're losing, you're losing your Vitamin C

DOKO E

Doko E is one of the very rare texts sang directly in Japanese. An extraordinary lyrical piece, which is in fact a mixture of Japanese radio and television commercials or catch phrases, punctuated by Damo Suzuki's own comments. The part which follows is the text of the extract featured on *Limited Edition* and later on *Unlimited Edition* followed by a copy of the original text in Japanese.

Literal translation does not evoke the powerful feeling of the text in its original tongue, but reads as follows:

Those filthy bloody factories in Tokyo.
It's just a polluted city, where can we go?
Discover Japan!
The pollution is making it more and more shitty.
For God's sake let's get away.
But where can we escape to?
This cold, filthy polluted city!
It's become so foul that...
Even the trees have withered away.
What's happened to them?
Clean people, clean rice, clean homes, clean earth — no chance.
Let's try eating fresh vegetables, but stop eating the fish.
Why?!!!?

DOKO E - Original Japanese Text

工場の汚染と東京と。

公害の町です、どこに行きましょう・

DISCOVER JAPAN !。

公害で汚くなった町です。

逃げましょう・どこへ、どこへ、どこへ、

どこへ逃げるの。

公害町、汚い町、寒い町。

いやです来ました、汚い町、そり…

木も何もなり・どこに行ったら。

きれいな人が、きれいな飯を、

きれいな家で、きれいな地面で、

きれいな野菜を食べてみて、食べて

みて・食べてみて―。

お魚の食べるの止めましょう。など。

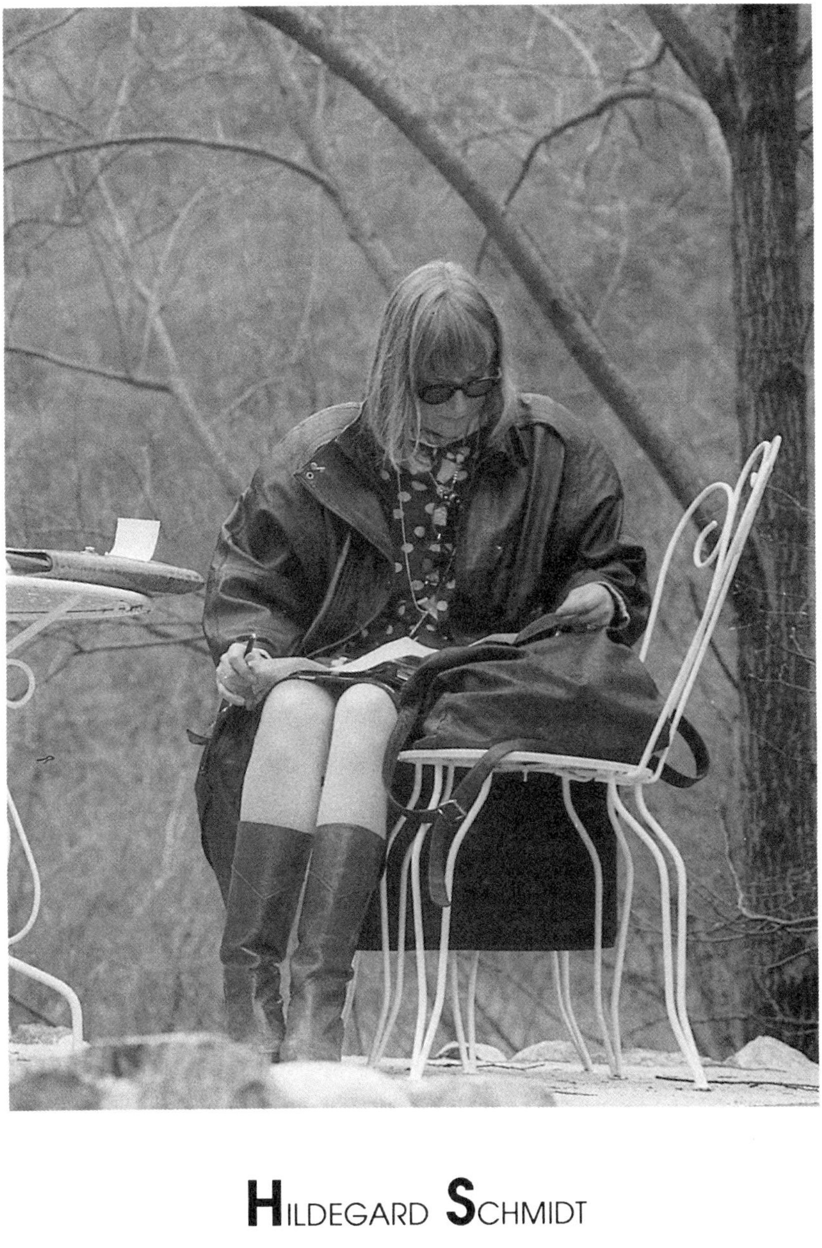

HILDEGARD SCHMIDT

SINCE 1971, HILDEGARD SCHMIDT HAS BEEN THE MANAGER of Can. She first met her future husband Irmin Schmidt when they were travelling in the same train compartment going to a music festival in East Germany:

> "I met Irmin when I was 17 years old. I thought I was going to become a 'Madame Chef d'Orchestre' but instead I became the manager of a rock band. And what a rock band!"

Hildegard has never assumed the role of manager as one usually means it in the rock business. She organises everything. She is not only busy with concerts, relations between the musicians and record companies, but also with tax and financial problems. For instance, she has always arranged that everyone be supplied with money without them having to worry about whether there was any or not available at that moment.

She has to all intents and purposes been a member of Can. She always gives her advice regarding the music, and never puts upon the group with the kind of arguments record companies commonly use such as, "make more commercial stuff". She has always believed in Can's way of working. She always considers her part as that of someone who represents the group as it is, and not as what someone else would have liked it to be — that to her is essential. For example, when the group made her listen to the tapes of *Tago Mago*, initially planned as a single LP, she persuaded them to make a double album when she heard pieces like *Peking O* and *Augmn*. They

Hildegard Schmidt has managed Can from 1971 to the present day.

thought the idea was mad, but finally the reaction the record received proved her right.

In 1980, Hildegard Schmidt recovered the rights to all the United Artists albums and she launched Spoon Records, a label specially designed for any product from the Can members. It is also she who has kept all the Can musicians in touch with each other when the group disbanded in 1978.

Since 1986, she has been involved in a partnership with the Swiss music production company Fink & Star Production A.G., (P.O. Box 108, CH 8031, Zürich), which has notably produced the last Irmin Schmidt albums *Musk At Dusk* and *Reporter*, and Can's return album.

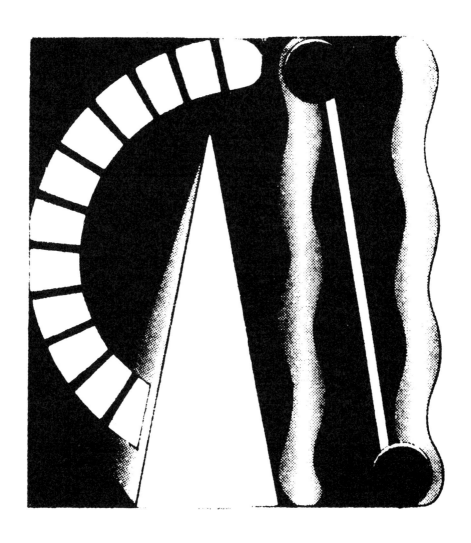

Can in the Studio

Can have always had a very special method of working in the studio, based on the idea of 'instant composing' as Jaki Liebezeit once put it. Similar to their live concerts, it very much depended on the magical interaction between the group as they were improvising. It is a form of improvisation which can sometimes stand as a real example of telepathy. The group are able to generate a mystical and magical atmosphere unrivalled by any other group of our time, reflecting an interest in the more direct elements of the mystical and the occult.

Some famous stories are known; Holger Czukay

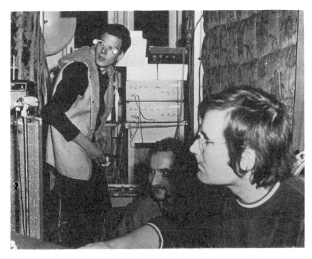

David Johnson, Holger Czukay and Irmin Schmidt recording in the first studio in Cologne.

communicating with plants, Jaki Liebezeit stopping the clocks of *The Old Grey Whistle Test* studio, Michael Karoli giving orders to an old organ in Weilerswist, Irmin Schmidt going to a fortune-teller to try and find out if Can would soon have a new singer... Michael Karoli:

"The magic side of Can? It's all in our improvising concept. It is the way the brain is working. Magic is when you find this way, the brain is making connections alone — that's magic. Magic is also a technique. You must be open, in a sense you must let the others play you. But there is a risk of being hurt. When you speak about magic, you lose it."

In the early days they sometimes double-tracked with only two stereo tape recorders, "There is no Can piece which is finished...", commented Irmin Schmidt. Rarely did they try higher levels of multi-tracking with this modest equipment. Michael Karoli's guitar was often double-tracked, as he could add another guitar track when flute was to be added by Jaki Liebezeit or Malcolm Mooney, for example. Despite this, conventional lead guitar lines were rare on Can's records and Michael Karoli often changed instruments like on *Outside My Door* where he adds the harmonica.

It was this interchangeable attitude towards their instruments that often contributed to the unique studio sound. For instance, when Jaki Liebezeit added to the texture, he seemed to move away from his standard drum kit, and added exotic percussion or a wind instrument. However, of all the members Irmin Schmidt was seemingly more obscure on record. Irmin Schmidt:

"I was learning to play rock music in those days, and I had a broken keyboard. The atmosphere on all the recordings of this early period was very spontaneous, nearly live recordings as with everything at that time. The process changed during the years, but we always sort of recorded live."

Until 1974 (up to and including the *Soon Over Babaluma* LP) Can recorded with two Revox machines, which meant that there were more risks than for other groups, with the added problems about mixing levels. Irmin Schmidt:

"When we recorded with this two track technique, there were sometimes a lot of mistakes in the mix. On *Future Days* the organ is not very well mixed, but it couldn't have been remixed - because it was on two track it couldn't be changed."

Michael Karoli:

"You don't have to play so loud in the studio — it's maybe even silly to do so."

Holger Czukay has always stressed the importance of building a relationship and understanding with the studio machinery:

"In a studio you make a concert for machines, and machines really like to listen. They have a heart and soul — they are living beings. The Can recordings are best when they are made under unusual circumstances and with an unusual technique. I would say when the desk and the equipment are treated like human beings. Like Jaki treats his drums, like his children."

When they gained a 16 track facility in 1975 (for recording the *Landed* LP), Can's music did not change much on record in terms of clarity, density or texture. Possibly their most complex creations were made with their old modest equipment, like *Pinch* or *Future Days*. Holger Czukay:

Can's first experiments at Schloss Norvenich in 1968.

"When we got this new equipment, I was no longer the only one responsible for technique. The recording was a lot better on a

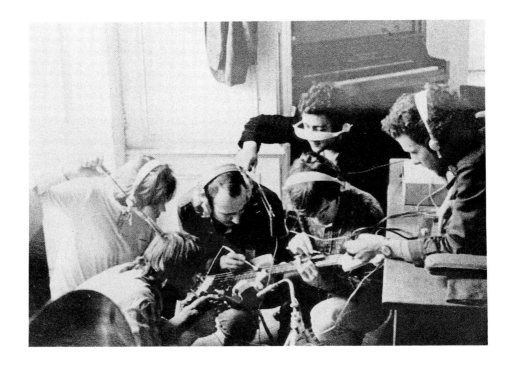

Michael Karoli,
Holger Czukay
and Irmin
Schmidt at the
time of
recording *Tago
Mago*.

technical level, but at the same time the music went in a different direction, away from our initial ideas."

Irmin Schmidt:

"In fact, we never had any plan, the plan was the group itself. Sometimes we played for two days in the studio, recording almost everything. Then we listened and when everybody liked it we worked on it. Sometimes we cut in the tape, sometimes we played it again. But even with the 16 track machine, the overdubs were spontaneous. Each of us would criticise the music, it is one important element of our collective way of working."

Their method of working and creating records, obviously meant that there was a lot of material that never found its way onto record. Can is certainly the only band where the unreleased music, both studio and live, is more important in quantity, and sometimes in quality as well, than the official recorded work. Michael Karoli:

"Holger guards the Can archives. Not counting the live tapes from the concerts, there are hundreds of hours of music lying around. For each record made, there was quite an amount of material left off, plus many of the sessions we did."

Holger Czukay:

"When I was the sound engineer of Can, all the music passed through my hands, I was controlling it. And when the music was 'edited' it was the same thing. Our records have many thousands of cuts, really."

By early 1976, a typical day at the Inner Space studio would take the following pattern. The group would begin to assemble in the studio at around 3.00 p.m., the process being completed around 6.00 p.m. Certain discussions would take place, drinks would be drunk, and so on. Overall the atmosphere would be full of ease and freedom from tension. Occasionally someone would wander over to an instrument and play it; it might or might not be his own one.

As the evening wore on, the amount of music played increased, as did the number of participants per session. One might find Michael Karoli on drums, Jaki Liebezeit on bass guitar, Holger Czukay on piano, Irmin Schmidt on congas and bongos, or any other possible combination of these. René Tinner would be responsible for recording what warranted being recorded on the MCI 16 track recorder, with Holger Czukay making occasional sound checks on the monitoring headphones.

Then would come an extended interval during which Holger Czukay would make a 2 track reduction and copy extracted highlights. As the night wore on, the probability of finding the individual members of Can at their normal posts would become progressively greater. And if someone suggested calling it a day at around 2.00 a.m. in the morning, then proceedings would be terminated.

Of course, that wouldn't necessarily be typical as there was no such thing as a typical Can recording session. However, one might wonder what Can's records would be like if they did not have these superb studio facilities freely available with their own space and no time limitations. It is difficult to imagine how they would have reacted to the pressures of studio recording at £300 per hour. Using their own studio has always been connected to a strong political attitude towards the music business. Irmin Schmidt:

"If we were recording in another studio other than ours, the "product" would be automatically manipulated. Record companies tend to think that good music can only be done with a certain technique and a big amount of money. It's absurd, and this kind of reasoning alienates the creativity of many musicians. In fact, the whole industry would go bankrupt if more bands recorded their music in their own studio. They would be able to control their music better, like we do and always did."

The musicians within Can were always inspired by many different kinds of music. In attempt to bring together some of these inspirations and to merge eclecticism with humour, at a very early stage they started recording a series of pieces that became to be known as the E.F.S. (Ethnological Forgery Series). Only a few of these pieces appeared on the records; five on *Unlimited Edition*, one on *Flow Motion*, and one on *Can*. These pieces could be based on African music, a theme from Offenbach, dixieland jazz, and so on. They were a set of musical deviations which were filled with irony and

More experiments at Schloss Norvenich.

encapsulated the whole spirit of Can. Holger Czukay:

"Yes, we began these forgeries very early, and sometimes it was very funny. Irmin, for example, was a great imitator of the Nō singers. As soon as he started singing in this Japanese way we would start laughing. I am sure Irmin could have succeeded in becoming a great opera star if he had gone on this way! On *Augmn* he has a very strange voice which I treated with a generator, which I could do as Jaki was playing the bass at the beginning. Irmin sang wonderfully... And we had a lot of fun during these times."

Irmin Schmidt:

"We never really had an E.F.S. concept. We invented the expression rather late, in fact many pieces in this style were already done. We were not making ethnic music at any price, we were making music, that's all. And one day, we found out that we had quite a few pieces with this strong ethnic influence, more than anywhere else.

We all listen to music from all over the world; Jaki is very interested in Arabian music, Holger particularly in Vietnamese music, and me, even before Can, I was enthusiastic about Japanese and African music. I even studied them at University. In fact, we invented the E.F.S. concept to enjoy ourselves, and I must say it's a fine phrase for all this part of our music. But this is not a real concept, it's an aspect of the whole Can concept. In a way, all Can pieces are E.F.S. The whole group is an E.F.S.!"

"In a studio you make a concert for machines, and machines really like to listen." Holger Czukay.

In addition to the far flung inspirations, it is interesting to note that apart from the German quartet, all the other members of Can were always from remote origins. Malcolm Mooney was a Black American, Damo Suzuki came from Japan (for many observers the group was at their best with these two, as each provided the group with inspiration in their own unique way), Rosko Gee from Jamaica, and Reebop from Ghana. Even when they were trying out new singers,

one of them, Raj, was from Indonesia.

Although many claim that Can were mainly a live band, they did produce many memorable moments in the studio as well. However, Can's records although relatively successful, never perhaps achieved the mainstream success that their creativity deserved. Holger Czukay:

> "Our relative lack of success...? Can's problems lay in creating too much, the whole structure was too dense and maybe it should have been thinned out."

Jean-Noël Ogouz, the former label manager at United Artists in France:

> "During the early '70s, Can had the chance to know someone who supported them in their record company in each European territory. We never really marketed them to any great extent, each album sold between twenty and thirty thousand — far better than the sales for Amon Düül II, for instance. We did get airplay for *Spoon*, that's all, and I remember having to fight to ensure that *Soon Over Babaluma* was released in France with its original silver cover."

Irmin Schmidt:

> "We did not sell millions of records so I cannot say that we reached the best audience. But in a way we did, because we touched around 40,000 people — they are certainly nice people but I would prefer that there were many more."

Although they never reached a very large audience, they were always a favourite of critics and other musicians alike. However, cover versions of Can pieces are very hard to find in other group's repertoires, doubtless because Can's tracks were so personal that they could only belong to them. Of the well-established bands, the Jesus And Mary Chain have dared a cover version, by giving their own rendition of *Mushroom* during their 1986 concerts. It was a modern but faithful version, both minimal and electric, which perfectly fitted in their shows. A live version, recorded in Nuremburg, can be found on their *Barbed Wire Kisses* compact-disc compilation from 1988 (Blanco Y Negro/WEA 242331-2). The song was a natural one for the group to cover, the Jesus and Mary Chain adding their then customary wall of feedback.

Outside of this, some isolated artists have tried to give their own tribute to Can. Loop have recorded a fairly faithful version of *Mother Sky*, about which Michael Karoli recently commented in *Melody Maker*, saying that merely duplicating the song must be ungratifying. The French poly-instrumentalist Thierry Müller covered *She Brings The Rain* under the pseudonym of Ruth (LP *Polaroid/Roman/Photo*, Paris-Album, DKF 3820, in 1985) and the band Complot Bronswick were reported in 1989 to be working on the same song for their upcoming album (on the Ikonaki Label). In East Germany, the East Berlin synthesizer singer/performer Jörg Thomasius has twice referred to Can. Firstly with his group Das Freie Orchester he did a live version of *Mother Sky* on December 27th, 1987 (cassette KK 011), and with Dieter Zobel (guitar, computer, voice) they included an African singer stolen from the radio in a piece called *Malcolm Makes The World Go Round*, an evident tribute to Can's first singer (Cassette *Musik Aus Dem Regen*, KK 007).

Today, the Can studio still exists in Weilerswist, although most of the time it is deserted by its founders, since even Holger Czukay works mostly in his own home studio. However, he still co-owns the Can studio with the group's chief sound-engineer René Tinner. Many musicians from Germany and Europe like to go there in search of an efficient and mystical place to work.

Lɪᴠᴇ Cᴀɴ

Anyone who ever witnessed can in concert (in whichever phase or line-up they appeared) will affirm that a rock group has rarely improvised so freely and extensively in front of an audience. Parallels may be drawn with early incarnations of Soft Machine, or Kraftwerk, with Matching Mole, some of the '70s Miles Davis groups, Fela Kuti from Africa, or the early Californian bands to name a few examples. But the 'improvisation' in these cases would lend itself to more modal, conventional uses of it, rather than being the overriding principal element of the musical construction itself, as it was with Can.

Especially in the early days, Can always refused to promote themselves or their 'product' live on any terms other then their own: i.e. total improvisation. Michael Karoli:

"For me, Can concerts are of equal importance to our records. On record we are four or five people working and trying to create something. With a concert it is the opposite, we have no deadline to work to, it's better. I have never practised a solo in my life and I never know what I'm going to play until I play it now!"

Holger Czukay:

"Whereas most musicians remake their records on stage, note-for-note, we come on stage without plans or preconceptions of what we are going to play exactly. Can's magic is when we are really good on stage."

Irmin Schmidt:

"Of course, if our records sounded like our concerts, people wouldn't go to the concerts - they would have heard it all on the records. In fact, the biggest difference between our live and recorded performances is Jaki."

Jaki Liebezeit:

"It's got a lot to do with the feeling. That feeling originates from the audience. If I like people, then I really start beating."

Irmin Schmidt:

"Nobody plays quite so differently in live performances as Jaki does. In the studio he always plays terribly precisely and in a cultivated way. On stage he seems to get carried away more."

But there are shades of the kettle calling the pot black here, the changes in style exhibited by Irmin Schmidt when on stage are perhaps even more dramatic. You only have to compare the subtlety shown by him on *Ege Bamyasi* against the live performances of the same time around 1973, to show the contrast. Irmin Schmidt could become almost demonic on stage without sparing the decibels. Irmin Schmidt:

"I had this Alpha 77, a very simple construction, in fact. Not really a synthesiser, but rather a sort of synthesiser of the first generation. At this time (around 1971) I especially wanted to have a very simple machine, to be able to change the sound of the organ, of the clavinet, and of the electric piano. I changed the sound of my old Farfisa. It was very old, in fact it had been built by an electronics maker in Zurich. On stage it was very efficient, I could visualise the plug connections very fast and then improvise without any preparation."

Can often made it a point of honour to advertise their concerts by putting up posters which stated that they were going to play for a longer time than most standard rock groups. In Paris in 1973, before the Olympia gig of November, Irmin Schmidt had said in various interviews that the group would play for at least four hours, therefore inciting curious people to come around... And one year later in London for the Hammersmith Palais concert in October, the bill clearly announced, "Can" and just below, "playing for three hours!"

Although many tried, few could succeed in describing in words that special moment one of their live concerts represented - never a musical routine, rather an arena for passion and excess. Although, there was never much movement on stage but the group knew how to make a theatrical use of contrasts both in volume and in sound

"On stage the connection between us is so strong, we get the influence from each to the other."
Irmin Schmidt.

quality. Again, in terms of Can, 'improvisation' (in the usual sense of the word as a jazz musician might use it) is rather a limiting word. For them it also denotes the ideas of advancing, exploring further, and taking off. On stage, Can built atmospheres, using themes from some of their 'songs' often only as landmarks, as pretexts and springboards from which to take off. Irmin Schmidt:

"We are really composing on stage. For example, we take the rhythm pattern of *Spoon* as a basis, and then we use it to create new things. Around 1975/6 our music became less 'improvised', and we began to play pieces that people asked for. For a long time we had never done it, and then we did, because it's very hard to resist that kind of pressure - "Play your tunes! Play your pieces!". But we then realised that it was not so bad to play definite pieces from time to time, because there was still places inside them for some new adventures. Also, when you have 'improvised' for a long time, you think, "Why not play real pieces now?", because it is a new experience. A new one, so an exciting and a stimulating one."

In a concert situation, the audience and their responses,

and any eventuality in the duration of the show, all played their part in the creation of the music. On their first British tour, in Bristol, the theatre manager discreetly informed each member of the band that they had to stop playing due to the bye-laws. They complied and left the stage one by one, save for Holger Czukay, who hadn't heard the instructions of the manager. Holger Czukay:

"After a while, I realised what was happening - I played softer and softer, ready to finish. The whole audience was really with us, very quiet, and then, in another room, somebody started playing the piano, so I answered the piano phrases, and this conversation went on for about ten minutes. It was more silence than anything but there was an incredible communication with real feeling between us and the audience, in fact the audience became real musicians! To have communication that strong was something completely new for me..."

However, because of the nature of the music and their way of improvising, some concerts contained elements of

"Can's magic is when we are really good on stage."
Holger Czukay.

provocation. Mal of Cabaret Voltaire:

"In a way they were like the Velvet Underground or The Doors, in that they didn't come across as hippies, there were more violent overtones - but like any of those groups, in reality it probably didn't exist.

However, I do remember seeing a Can gig once in Bradford and things weren't going as planned and they got quite aggressive. It was nice to see that harder edge to it... I think they transcended a lot of the 'woolly hat' hippy aspects. For example, I could never see them in the same light as Gong!"

It is true that the group could produce some of their best moments when under great adversity, such as when their equipment failed (as happened in many of the early gigs with Malcolm Mooney), or when a guitar was stolen (as happened once at Croydon). Michael Karoli:

"When things are against us, we can't afford to play badly - it's like the concept of the blind navigator or the one-armed Japanese fighter."

Some other occurrences during their concerts were sometimes more dramatic, but always incorporated into the event. Jaki Liebezeit overcame a twenty minute power cut in Brussels by nonchalantly drumming on regardless in the darkness. And in Bordeaux, a maniac appeared on stage brandishing a knife - and threatening to use it unless the band played a third encore. Not surprisingly, they complied.

These events were obviously fairly unique examples, but on a good night, with an enthusiastic audience, Can would be inspired and encouraged by them to give their best performances. Can would always be sensitive to audience reaction. They would look for a response in the same way that a comic looks for feedback from his audience. Can undoubtedly fed off a good responsive audience and individually among themselves. As Irmin Schmidt put it, "The connection between us is so strong, we get the influence from each to the other."

Holger Czukay says that his greatest desire is to please the audience and to have them participate, but to cause them to dance is a far greater achievement than to cause them to applaud. It is not surprising that some of the group's best performances were at dance venues; the Mayfair Ballroom in Newcastle, the Lyceum, and most notably the Hammersmith Palais in London and the Bataclan in Paris.

Save one isolated concert in Belgium, two in Austria, and on the last tour, in '77, visits to Switzerland, Spain and Portugal, Can only toured regularly in Germany, France and Britain. Irmin Schmidt:

"It is very hard to classify the audiences of these countries, they are all different. But doubtless in France there are more contrasts. I remember the very aggressive mood in Grenoble, the very tense one of the Bataclan in Paris, the very inventive and calm one in Arles in the old Roman theatre. I would very much like to have a good tape of the Arles gig, it could have been suitable for a 'live' Can album...

Also, the atmospheres were different depending on whether we had a singer or not. Personally, I think it is better to have a singer because the relationship with the audience is then more direct, the human voice is more personal and more direct than an instrument. With Can there were always these periods; a singer, then no singer, then a singer again, and so on. Sometimes Michael sang as well, but he is not a lead singer, he is not the type. He puts vocals inside the music, but he never tried nor wanted to be the 'lead singer' of the group."

Obviously, Can should have released at least one 'live' album, as many of their concerts revealed specific styles not found on any of their records or, indeed, necessarily repeated at another concert. Such examples of classic Can concerts are Colchester '72, Edinburgh '73, Nanterre '74. Concerts in '75 in Paris at the Bataclan and Chaillot. Also, in '75 at Colchester, Brighton, Siegendorf and Arles, and in '76 in Brussels, Grenoble and London, and in '77 in Cologne. Irmin Schmidt:

"For me, Can concerts are of equal importance to our records."
Michael Karoli.

"The real reason why we never released a 'live' album is that all our records are more or less 'live' in the studio. Regarding a real 'live' record, we sort of missed our chance, because there was a time when we had this certain style, and this kind of thing never comes back, especially ten or twelve years later. I was talking about Arles, but I remember very violent gigs long before that in

England.

At the time we weren't objective enough to judge and always thought that we could do better; but we did not do better, we changed, became different. And different does not mean 'better' or 'not better', it means different, that's it. At that time, 1972/3, we were very sincere and unpretentious, it was very spontaneous on stage. Nobody on stage, or on record either, for that matter, pretended to be someone he was not. It was a very important thing.

Now, to compile a 'live' album would be an incredible task. We would have to listen to the hundreds of hours of tapes we have, which is impossible for active musicians. We would also have to agree on a choice of tracks, which would be very difficult as well. It would take at least six months for everyone to do that. We have a mountain of 'live' cassettes, which vary in sound quality from the bad to the excellent, but we used to record all our concerts.

Sometimes we used to listen to them afterwards, and we discussed a few points. But in fact nobody in the group ever listened back to everything. When we were on tour, it was impossible to listen back each night to the previous evening's gig, only Reebop was doing that at the end, he spent whole nights listening to cassettes and was able to find a few details, it was crazy! Yes, that is the main problem for a possible 'live' album; these five hundred hours of music which are lying around that we would have to go through..."

Can Reunion

IT WAS ALMOST INNEVITABLE THAT CAN WOULD MAKE SOME music again together, "Being so conspicuous by their absence", as Steve Lake commented in the *Melody Maker* of May 22nd, 1981. Rarely, have a group dared to take such a risk — getting together in their original format 18 years after their debut, and 17 years after one of them had left the group.

Early in 1986, Holger Czukay, Irmin Schmidt, Jaki Liebezeit and Michael Karoli all agreed to make another record. To complete their line-up they had the idea of working with both Malcolm Mooney and Damo Suzuki, but the latter refused, saying that, "For me, Can belong to the past", and explaining that he was now involved in new things.

However, the contact with Malcolm Mooney was very telepathic. Irmin Schmidt:

"I went back from Germany to Rousillon and I began to writing a letter to Malcolm. One or two days later, I had not even finished the letter and I received a letter from him saying, "After all these years, why don't we make another record?" Of course, we were always in contact with each other, but there was always maybe a year or so between letters or telephone calls and even then we never talked about music. So, it was clear, it had to happen!"

The meeting with Malcolm, who came over from New York, was important for all of them, and a very special event in the life of Can. Holger Czukay:

"I wasn't at all surprised. He came quite clear in his mind, he never lost his power. However, one thing surprised me about him — he showed much more of a sense of humour. The older people get, the more they see everything a little bit easier."

Irmin Schmidt:

"We played immediately, and we did not have the feeling that we had not seen him for such a long time. It was as if he had left only a year ago..."

So, they all met at the Outer Space Studio in December 1986 and they played together for a few weeks and several hours of music were laid down. The rumours and anticipation that a brand new Can product was on its way began to grow in the music business. In Spring 1988, the five musicians met again at the Outer Space studio for the shooting of a documentary film about the group, made by a video team from Austria. In the New Musical Express of March 3rd, 1989, a source claims that the group has signed to Big Life, the label of the 'house' music star Yazz, an idea which has been suggested because of Hildegard Schmidt's strong involvement in Yazz's management. After much speculation, a world-wide deal is finalised with Phonogram on May 31st, 1989, with the long-awaited Can product to be released in the September of the same year, under the double-meaning title of *Rite Time*.

Obviously, the reunion (or more accurately, the first coming together for the whole group) of the five original members was not so easy for everyone. Holger Czukay:

"I immediately felt the same tension, as in our worst times, but we had the common feeling of really wanting to make something together. For me, this Can revival is of course only one of the things I'm doing. What will happen in the future I can't really say. When I am with Can again, I feel like a member of Can, but if I was working alone everything would be much easier, I could easily avoid unnecessary discussions. Sometimes I don't like it at all, I wish I could go on working by myself instead of having to listen to some opinions which do not count for me at all. But, I consider that as a new experience, because I never did something twice in my life.

This time I did it as a favour to our manager because I knew she was really looking forward to it. But that was not easy, I had to really compromise a lot, very much more than the others. I didn't really want to play bass, it was a declaration of war like in the late '70s days, so I shared the bass with Micky. I also played French horn, and I put some music from the dictaphone which is a special thing because all the loops and the musical information are somehow recorded and you have to get the right logic to combine all the things into one musical form which makes sense.

It is important that the mood is not against the music which is coming into existence."

Irmin Schmidt smiles:

"We must accept Holger. He has always been a bit strange. Let us say that this time his strangeness was more integrated than at certain times..."

Jaki Liebezeit, also, had to overcome his current aversion to the bass guitar, but the fact that Malcolm Mooney was there certainly helped him to feel comfortable. Jaki Liebezeit:

"*Monster Movie* was the best record, because of the singing, and I found that again there, it's easy to play drums when Malcolm starts singing. Damo has of course different qualities but Malcolm makes me play so easily, with him the rhythm is so strong from inside."

As usual, Can worked in a very relaxed way, and it's sure that down in the South of France near Nice in the calm atmosphere of Michael Karoli's studio and house, they had never been so far away from commercial pressure. Michael Karoli:

"When the sessions were finished, we worked in a slow way on the tapes. In 1987 and 1988, me and Holger met again at various opportunities and I did the backing vocals. I also supplied some bass guitar (sometimes on the same pieces that Holger did) and some pocket organ, and the two of us worked on the editing and the mix. In fact, we have so much material over, exactly like in the old days, that we could maybe release a second album from the sessions, but nothing is sure yet."

Holger Czukay:

"Of course, I dealt with the tapes as I ever did, but this time I did it together with Micky, and we both got along very well about that. It was more or less a cleaning up or building up form, so that the band at the end really sounds like a band and not like a computer production."

As ever with Can there was always the risk that things could have turned out in a bad way. Irmin Schmidt:

"If it had not worked, it would not have been a catastrophe, but it would not have proved anything either."

But as it turned out, the spirit of the group was still very much there. Holger Czukay:

"Yes, there was a danger in trying to recreate old things. But we found that even now we are all doing things separately, Can didn't loose its spontaneity, Can recovered in terms of being more spontaneous. Twenty years ago it was a big excitement. Now, it's a lot more fun, but it's definitely a special moment."

Irmin Schmidt:

"It was not the same spirit as that of twenty years ago, because twenty years have passed. But the spirit was very good, despite the fact that it was not the same discovery, I mean this 1968 vision. And now we are not consciously in the avant-garde, we just do what we feel, in a simple way."

Of course, the strength of the challenge of making new music together is in relation to the mighty sound of the music, and perhaps the return inevitably disappoints expectations. Can cannot pretend anymore to be ahead of its time (nobody can do that for more than a few years, especially as they have already been so strongly creative), but

Rite Time is definitely in tune with the late '80s as well as a continuation from their material of the late '60s and '70s. Malcolm Mooney now has a cleaner image, his interesting blues voice has developed from the *Monster Movie* days to a more condensed sound which is at once "cannesque", with flashes of deep inspiration which hint at the runaway exploration and genius of the '68/69 period but with a more sophisticated texture. On the whole, the music is much more produced than spontaneous, which is highlighted by the length of the pieces which are shorter than the older epic pieces like *Yoo Doo Right* from 1969 or *Animal Waves* from 1977. "It's definitely Can music", says Irmin Schmidt without a second of hesitation, "and the rest depends on the journalists..."

Holger Czukay agrees:

"The music is difficult to describe, but it is without doubt Can music in the old terms, but packed and presented as you have to do it in these days. It's genuine, and the sound is good as well, because the technology has advanced since Can began in the late '60s."

However, the new material is probably best summed up by Malcolm Mooney:

"The old Can sound is still there only with new ideas — it still has a Can foundation. It's like they used to have manual can openers now they have these automatic ones — it's a bit like that with the music — it is a very good feeling."

Although it is generally accepted that Can have not reunited as a real group (they live in three different countries and they have not really played together since the December 1986 session wich gave birth to *Rite Time*), the question of possible live concerts is again the subject of speculation. Hildegard Schmidt has talked of "a few eventual gigs in big cities like London, Paris, Berlin, to push the record if it would help", but nothing is sure and the musicians themselves don't share the same opinion about such a plan. Holger Czukay:

"I personally really wanted that, more then making a record. Because records I can do myself, but I can't play live by myself. I mean I could do it, but it would take too much technology. There is also the fact that on stage, a band makes sense. But the others were against it, they didn't like the idea at all, and so we made an album."

Irmin Schmidt:

If I go on stage again, it would have to be something quite strong, it would have to be a real creation, like it was with Can in the '70s. I might come on stage again for my opera..."

Maybe it is Jaki Liebezeit, although always ready to play on stage or in the studio in many different contexts, who best sums up the situation:

"Now, Can is like James Bond. When James Bond makes a new film, he doesn't need to do a tour. It's the same with us; we made a new record, we don't need to do a tour..."

DISCOGRAPHY

(D) German release, (GB) UK release, (F) French release, (J) Japanese release

CAN

1968

KAMA SUTRA (PARTS 1/2) Single by Irmin Schmidt (sic). Metronome M25-128 (D).

1969

MONSTER MOVIE (LP) *Father Cannot Yell, Mary Mary So Contrary, Outside My Door, Yoo Doo Right.* Music Factory SRS 001 (D). Re-released on United Artists. Re-released on Spoon Records in 1981, SPOON 004 (D). Re-released on compact disc May 1989, Spoon CD 004. In USA, D21S-75415.

1970

THIEF Track featured on the double-album sampler *Electric Rock*. Liberty LBS 83372/3 (D).

THE CAN SOUNDTRACKS (LP) *Deadlock, Tango Whiskyman,* (both from the movie *Deadlock*), *Don't Turn The Light On, Leave Me Alone* (from the movie *Cream*), *Soul Desert* (from the movie *Mädchen Mit Gewalt*), *Mother Sky* (from the movie *Deep End*), *She Brings The Rain* (from the movie *Bottom — Ein Grober Graublauer Vogel*). Liberty LBS 83437 (D). Re-released in 1981 on Spoon Records: SPOON 005 (D). Re-released on compact disc in May 1989, Spoon CD 005. In USA, D21S-75416.

SOUL DESERT/SHE BRINGS THE RAIN (Single) Liberty 15340 (D).

1971

TAGO MAGO (Double LP) *Paperhouse, Mushroom, Oh Yeah, Hallelujah, Augmn, Peking O, Bring Me Coffee Or Tea.* Liberty UAS 29211/12 (D). Re-relased in 1981 on Spoon: SPOON 006/7 (D). Re-released on compact disc in May 1989, Spoon CD 006/7. In USA, D22V-75417.

TURTLES HAVE SHORT LEGS/HALLELUJAH (Single) Liberty 15465 (D).

SPOON/SHIKAKU MARU TEN (Single)Liberty 35304 (D).

1972

VITAMIN C/I'M SO GREEN (Single) United Artists 35472A (D).

EGE BAMYASI (LP) *Pinch, Sing Swan Song, One More Night, Vitamin C, Soup, I'm So Green, Spoon.* United Artists 29414 (D). Re-released in 1981 on Spoon Records: SPOON 008 (D). Re-released on compact disc in May 1989, Spoon CD 008. In USA, D21S-75418.

1973

SPOON/I'M SO GREEN (Single) United Artists (GB).

FUTURE DAYS (LP) *Future Days, Spray, Moonshake, Bel Air.* United Artists UAS 29505 1 (D). Re-released in 1981 on Spoon Records: SPOON 009 (D). Re-released on compact disc in May 1989, Spoon CD 009. In USA, D21S-75149.

MOONSHAKE/FUTURE DAYS (Single) United Artists 355 96A (D).

1974   *LIMITED EDITION* (LP) *Gomorha, Doko E, LH 702 (Nairobi-München), I'm Too Leise, Musette, Blue Bag (Inside Paper), EFS No 27, TV Spot, EFS No 7, The Empress And The Ukraine King, EFS No 10, Mother Upduff, EFS No 36.* United Artists USP 103 (GB). Limited edition of 15,000 copies.

SOON OVER BABALUMA (LP) *Dizzy Dizzy, Come Sta La Luna, Splash, Chain Reaction, Quantum Physics.* United Artists 29673 1 (D). Re-released in 1981 on Spoon Records: SPOON 010 (D). Re-released on compact disc in May 1989, Spoon CD 010. In USA, D21S-75420.

DIZZY DIZZY/SPLASH (Single) United Artists 35749A (D/GB).

1975   *THE CLASSIC GERMAN ROCK SCENE - CAN (1968-1972)* (LP) *Father Cannot Yell, Mary Mary So Contrary, Outside My Door, Mother Sky, She Brings The Rain, Peking O, Bring Me Coffee Or Tea, Vitamin C, Soup, I'm So Green, Spoon.* United Artists UAS 29 772/73 XB (D).

LANDED (LP) *Full Moon On The Highway, Half Past One, Hunters And Collectors, Vernal Equinox, Red Hot Indians, Unfinished.* Virgin V2041 (GB), Harvest 1C 062-29600 (D). Re- released on compact disc in June 1987, Virgin CDV2041. Scheduled re-release on CD, Spoon CD 25.

HUNTERS AND COLLECTORS/VERNAL EQUINOX (Single) Harvest 1C 006-31392 (D).

1976   *UNLIMITED EDITION (1968-1975)* (Double LP) Same track listing as *Limited Edition* with the addition of; *Cutaway, Connection, Fall Of Another Year, EFS No 8, Transcendental Express, Ibis.* Harvest 1 C148-29 653/54 (D). Virgin Caroline CAD 3001 (GB). Scheduled re-release on compact disc, Spoon CD 23/24.

OPENER (1971-1974) (Compilation LP) *Dizzy Dizzy, Moonshake, Sing Swan Song, Come Sta La Luna, Spoon, I'm So Green, Vitamin C, Future Days.* Sunset Records SLS 50400 (GB).

FLOW MOTION (LP) *I Want More, Cascade Waltz, Laugh Till You Cry - Live Till You Die, (O.R.N.), ...And More, Babylonian Pearl, Smoke (EFS No 59), Flow Motion.* Virgin VS 153 (GB), Harvest 1C 062-31837 (D). Re-released on compact disc in June 1987, Virgin CDV2071. Scheduled re-release on CD, Spoon CD 27.

I WANT MORE/...AND MORE (Single) Virgin VS 153 (GB), Virgin 640088-1 (F) Harvest (D).

SILENT NIGHT/CASCADE WALTZ (Single) Virgin VS 166 (GB), Harvest (D).

1977   *SAW DELIGHT* (LP) *Don't Say No, Sunshine Day And Night, Call Me, Animal Waves, Fly By Night.* Harvest 1C 064-32 156 (D), Virgin V2079 (GB).

DON'T SAY NO/RETURN (Single) Harvest IC 006-32155 (D).

1978   *OUT OF REACH* (LP) *Serpentine, Pauper's Daughter And I, November, Seven Days Awake, Give Me No "Roses", Like INOBE GOD, One More Day.* EMI Electricola LIP 4-A (GB). Harvest IC 066-32715 (D). Re- released on compact disc in 1988, Magnum/Thunderbolt CDTB025.

CANNIBALISM 1968-197 (Double LP) *Father Cannot Yell, Soul Desert, Soup, Mother Sky, She Brings The Rain, Mushroom, One More Night, Spray, Outside My Door, Chain Reaction, Hallelujah, Aumgn, Dizzy Dizzy, Yoo Doo Right.* United Artists UDM 105/6 (GB).

1979   *CAN* (LP) *All Gates Open, Safe, Sunday Jam, Sodom, A Spectacle, EFS No 99 "Can Can", Ping Pong, Can Be.* Harvest 1C 066-45-099 (D). Re-released on compact disc in 1986, under the title *Inner Space*, with *Can Can* and *Ping Pong* reversed in order, Magnum/Thunderbolt CDTB020. Scheduled re-release on CD with its original title, Spoon CD 28.

1980   *CANNABILISM* (Double LP) Same track listing as the original *Cannibalism* album, only *Spoon* replaces *Chain Reaction*. Spoon 001/2(D). Re-released on compact disc in May 1989 under the title *Cannibalism I*, with *Soul Desert* and *Spray* missing, Spoon CD 001/2. In USA, D22V- 75414.

Two other volumes of the *Cannibalism* series are planned on compact disc, *Cannibalism II* devoted to Can between 1974 and 1978 (Spoon CD 21/22), and *Cannibalism III* devoted to the solo records of Can members (Spoon CD 29/30).

SPOON/SILENT NIGHT (Single) Line Records 6. 12936 AC (D).

1981   *INCANDESCENCE (1969-1977)* (LP) *I Want More, Full Moon On The Highway, Gomorrah, Hunters And Collecters, The Empress And The Ukraine King, Mother Upduff, Call Me, Half Past One, Laugh Till You Cry... Live Till You Die, EFS No 36.* Virgin OVED 3 (GB).

ROCK IN DEUTSCHLAND - VOL 6 - CAN (LP) *Dizzy Dizzy, Moonshake, Sing Swan Song, Come Sta La Luna, Vitamin C, Future Days, I'm So Green, Pinch.* Strand LC 5830.

I WANT MORE/...AND MORE (Single) Virgin VS 422 (GB).

I WANT MORE/...AND MORE/SILENT NIGHT (Maxi Single) Virgin VS 422-12 (GB).

DELAY 1968 (1968-1969) (LP) *Butterfly, Pnoom, Nineteenth Century Man, Thief, Man Named Joe, Uphill, Little Star Of Bethlehem.* Spoon Records: SPOON 012 (D). Re-released on compact disc in May 1989, Spoon CD 012. In USA, D21S-75421.

1982   *ONLY YOU* (Cassette) *Mister Schmidt, Machine Dance II, Comment/Brain, Alone, Comment/Commercial, Spanish Drive, Comment/Axe, End Of A Party,*

Comment/Influence, Under The Surface, Comment Cheers, Only You One, Comment/Art, Comment/Finger, Shall I Get You More, Comment/God, A Radio Beam, Comment/Hands, Machine Dance I, Howdooyoudooright, Comment/Musician, The Can Telefon Jingle, Only You Two, The Master And The Needle, Rose, Comment/Next LP, Harry/Thief. Pure Freude PF23 (D). Limited Edition of 100 numbered copies cassette, packaged in a tin.

1983   *MOONSHAKE/TURTLES HAVE SHORT LEGS/ONE MORE NIGHT* (Maxi Single) Cherry Red 12" - CHERRY 57 (GB).

1984   *PREHISTORIC FUTURE(The Very First Session)* (Cassette) Tago Mago TM 4755 (F). Limited Edition of 2,000 copies.

1989   *RITE TIME* (LP/CD) *On The Beautiful Side Of A Romance, The Withoutlaw Man, Below This Level (Patient's Song), Movin' Right Along, Like A New Child, Hoolah Hoolah, Give The Drummer Some.* CD contains extra track, *In The Distance Lies The Future.* Phonogram 838 883 (LP) 1, (CD) 2, (Cassette) 4.

SUNDRIES

Most of the original United Artists albums (*Monster Movie, Soundtracks, Tago Mago, Ege Bamyasi, Future Days, Soon Over Babaluma*) were released in Germany, France and England, generally under the same catalogue number. *Ege Bamyasi, Future Days,* and *Soon Over Babaluma* (album: UA-LA343-G, cassette: UA-EA343-G) have been released in the United States. In Japan, three albums were released at the same time as the European originals: *Tago Mago* (Liberty LP-93025B), *Ege Bamyasi* (Liberty LLP-80759), and *Cannibalism* (United Artists GXC 79/80).

In France, *Landed* appeared on Barclay (840096), *Flow Motion* and *Saw Delight* on Polydor, *Out Of Reach* on Pathé-Marconi, and *Can* on Freebird (FLY 07). In England, *Out Of Reach* was released on Lightning (LIP 4) and *Can* on Laser (LASL 2), both through W.E.A. In Japan, *Landed* (VIP-4072), *Flow Motion* (VIP-4155) and *Saw Delight* (VIP-4104) were on Virgin.

The first Spoon re-releases included, *Monster Movie, Soundtracks, Tago Mago, Ege Bamyasi, Future Days, Soon Over Babaluma,* as well as *Cannibalism* and *Delay 1968,* were all licensed in France, Italy and Japan.

Soul Desert and *Oh Yeah* appeared on a German sampler. *Sing Swan Song, Mother Sky, One More Night* appeared on the double United Artists sampler LP (UAS 29697/98 XD (D). *Sing Swan Song* was featured on *Cosmic Kraut Hits, Vol 1* (Sunset SLS 50391), *Mother Sky* and *One More Night* on *Cosmic Kraut Hits, Vol 2* (Sunset SLS 50392), both French albums. On the English pressing of *Future Days, Bel Air* was called *Spare A Light. I Want More* appeared on the English compilation *Methods Of Dance* (Virgin OVEDC 5/1981) and was also featured on the *Hi-Voltage* cassette released in 1987 by the English rock weekly New Musical Express (NME 028).

All Can compact discs on Spoon are licensed and marketed by the London-based Mute Records worldwide, except in Germany and in France where Teldec Import Service and Mantra Records/Wotre Music are respectively the exclusive distributors. In the USA, the whole Spoon CD catalogue is released via Mute on the Enigma Retro label, and cassette versions of each CD are available. *Monster Movie* (D41G-75415), *Soundtracks* (D41G- 75416), *Tago Mago* (D41M-75417), *Ege Bamyasi* (D41G-75418), *Future Days* (D41G-75419), *Soon Over Babaluma* (D41G-75420), *Delay 1968* (D41G-75421) and *Cannibalism I* (D41M-75414) were the first to be issued in May 1989.

HOLGER CZUKAY

1969   *CANAXIS 5* (LP with Rolf Dammers) *Boat Woman Song, Canaxis*. Music Factory SRS 002 (D). Re-released on Spoon Records: SPOON 015 (D) in 1981.

1979   *MOVIES* (LP) *Cool In The Pool, Oh Lord Give Us More Money, Persian Love, Hollywood Symphony*. Electrola 1C 064-45- 754 (D), EMI EMC 3319 (GB), Trio AW 25007 (J).

1980   *LES VAMPYRETTES* (Maxi Single with Conny Plank and Axel Gros) *Biomutanten, Menetekel*. Electrola F 667.226 (D).

1981   *HOW MUCH ARE THEY?* (Maxi Single with Jaki Liebezeit and Jah Wobble) *How Much Are They?, Where's The Money?, Trench Warfare, Twilight World*. Island 12WIP 6701 (GB).

ON THE WAY TO THE PEAK OF NORMAL (LP) *Ode To Perfume, On The Way To The Peak Of Normal, Witches' Multiplication Table, Two Bass Shuffle, Hiss 'N' Listen*. Electrola 1C 064-46 400 (D), EMI EMC 3394 (GB), Trio AW 25013 (J).

ODE TO PERFUME/PERSIAN LOVE (Single) EMI 5280 (GB).

PHEW (LP with Phew, Jaki Liebezeit and Conny Plank) *Closed, Signal, Doze, Dream, Mapping, Aqua, P-Adic, Fragment, Circuit*. Pass Records 3F-28002 (J).

1982   *PERSIAN LOVE/COOL IN THE POOL* (Single) Trio AW-710 (J).

FULL CIRCLE (LP with Jaki Liebezeit and Jah Wobble)*How Much Are They?, Where's The Money?, Full Circle (RPS No 8), Trench Warfare, Twilight World*. Virgin 205 866-320 (D), Trio AW-25026 (J).

1983   *SNAKE CHARMER* (Mini LP with Jah Wobble and The Edge)*Snake Charmer, Hold On To Your Dreams, It Was A Camel, Sleazy, Snake Charmer (reprise)*. Island 205-969-270 (D), Island 818 010-1 (F).

1984   *DER OSTEN IST ROT (THE EAST IS RED)* (LP) *The Photo Song, Bänkel Rap '82, Michy, Rhönrad, Collage, Esperanto Socialiste, Der Osten Ist Rot, Das Massenmedium, Schaue Vertrauensvoll In Die Zukunft, Träum Mal Wieder*. Virgin

206 258-620 (D), Virgin 70240 (F), Virgin V2307 (GB).

A MESSAGE FROM HOLGER CZUKAY (Maxi single promotional use only, one side). Virgin CZ 1 (GB).

THE PHOTO SONG/DAS MASSENMEDIUM (Single) Virgin VS 671 (GB). Also a Maxi single (same as above plus *Biomutanten*): Virgin VS 671-12.

1987   *ROME REMAINS ROME* (LP) *Hey Baba Reebop, Blessed Easter, Sudetenland, Hit Hit Flop Flop, Perfect World, Music In The Air.* Virgin V2408 (GB). The compact disc edition of *Rome Remains Rome* (Virgin CDV2408) also contains excerpts from *Der Osten Is Rot (The East Is Red): Das Maasenmedium, The Photo Song, Rhönrad, Michy, Esperanto Socialiste, Träum Mal Wieder.*

Hey Baba Reebop was also featured on the *Hi- Voltage* cassette released in 1987 by the English rock weekly New Musical Express (NME 028).

1988   *PLIGHT AND PREMONITION* (LP/CD David Sylvian and Holger Czukay) Venture/Virgin CDVE 11.

1989   *FLUX - MUTABILITY* (LP/CD David Sylvian and Holger Czukay) Venture/Virgin CDVE 43.

Holger Czukay also appears on various records by Alex, Cluster, Cluster & Eno, Eurythmics, Phantom Band, Irmin Schmidt, David Sylvian, and SYPH. The piece *Persian Love* has appeared on two compilation albums; the Japanese *Snakeman Show* (Alfa Records ALR-28027, 1981) and the double LP *Music And Rhythm (WEA K 68 045, 1982).*

MICHAEL KAROLI

1984   *DELUGE* (LP with Polly Eltes) *One Thing (Or The Other), Fear Of Losing Control, Home Truths, Sentimental, The Lake, Deluge (The River).* Spoon Records SPOON 016 (D).

Michael Karoli also appears on various albums by Holger Czukay and Irmin Schmidt.

JAKI LIEBEZEIT

1980   *PHANTOM BAND* (LP by Phantom Band) *You Inspired Me, I'm The One, For M, Phantom Drums, Absolutely Straight, Rolling, Without Desire, No More Fooling, Pulsar, Latest News.* Sky Records SKY 048 (D).

1981   *FREEDOM OF SPEECH* (LP by Phantom Band) *Freedom Of Speech, EF 1, Brain Police, No Question, Relax, Gravity, Trapped Again, Experiments, Dream Machine, Dangerous Conversation.* Sky Records SKY 065 (D).

1984   *NOWHERE* (LP by Phantom Band) *Loading Zone, Planned Obsolescence, Mind Probe, Morning Alarm, Weird Love, Neon Man, Positive Day, Nervous Breakdown, The Party, The Space Monster, This Is The Rule, Cricket Talk, Nowhere.* Spoon Records SPOON 017 (D).

Jaki Liebezeit also appears on various records by Alex, Holger Czukay, Gabi Delgado, Brian Eno, Eurythmics, The Manfred Schoof Quartet, Gianna Mannini, Phew, Plaza Hotel, Michael Rother, Irmin Schmidt, Richard Schneider Junior and Jah Wobble.

IRMIN SCHMIDT

1980   *FILMMUSIK (1978-1981)* (LP extracts from soundtracks) *Im Herzen Des Hurrican, Der Tote Bin Ich, and Messer Im Kopf.* Spoon Records SPOON 003 (D).

1981   *TOY PLANET* (LP with Bruno Spoerri) *The Seven Game (Ring Of Smile - Reversed), Toy Planet, Two Dolphins Go Dancing, Yom Tov, Springlite Right, Rapido De Noir (Last Train To Eternity), When The Waters Comes To Life.* Spoon Records SPOON 011 (D). Re-released on compact disc in June 1989 (Venture/Virgin CDVE 48).

FILMMUSIK VOL. 2 (1981) (LP of extracts soundtracks) *Endstation Freiheit, Flächenbrand, Die Heimsuchung Des Assistenten Jung.* Spoon Records SPOON 013 (D).

1983   *ROTE ERDE (Originalmusik zur Fernsehserie - 1983)* (LP) *Rote Erde (Titelmelodie), Käthe Verbrennt Den Traume Vom Glück, Widerstand (I), Heimkehr, Undertage, Pauline, Trauermusik, Widerstand (II), Schwarze Tage, Zuhause, Abschied.* Teldec 6.25687 (AP) (D).

1984   *FILMMUSIK VOL. 3 & 4 (1981-1983)* (LP of extracts from soundtracks) *Flight To Berlin, Ruhe Sanft Bruno, Leben Gundlings..., Der Mann Auf Der Mauer, Es Ist Nicht Aller Tage Abend.* Spoon Records SPOON 018/19 (D).

1985   *HERR SCHMIDT* (Maxi single) Virgin Records 602047213 (D).

1987   *ROLL ON, EUPHRATES/YOU MAKE ME NERVOUS* (Maxi Single) WEA 248579-0 (D).

MUSK AT DUSK (LP) *Cliff Into Silence, Love, Roll On Euphrates, The Great Escape, Villa Wunderbar, The Child In History, Alcool.* WEA 242010 (LP), 242010-2 (CD), 242010-4 (cassette) (D/F).

1989   *REPORTER* (LP) *Zu Nah Dran, Gesicht Im Dunkel, Mountain Way, Rita's Tune, Nuts 'n' News, Bohemian Step, Geld Und Glister, Zocker.* Virgin/Venture 209 919 630.

Irmin Schmidt also appears on Holger Czukay's *Movies*.

DAMO SUZUKI

Records by Dunkelziffer featuring Damo Suzuki avaialble on the German label Fünf Und Viersig: LP *In The Night* (EfA 12- 4502, 1984), single *I See Your Smile/Q* (EfA 32-4503, 1984), maxi-single *You Make Me Happy* (EfA 12-4510, 1985).

CAN ON FILM

BEAT CLUB German television broadcast from 1971 with *Paperhouse*.

CAN FREE CONCERT 50 minute film by Peter Przygodda featuring extracts from the concert at the Cologne Sporthalle (February 3rd, 1972) plus studio recordings.

POP 2 March 22nd 1973: French television broadcast from a concert at the Bataclan in Paris.

Also:

1988: Documentary video (60 minutes) produced by Doro Film, Hannes Rossacher, 8 Winckelmannstrasse, 1150 Vienna, Austria.

Krieg der Töne 1987/88: Video (60 minutes) with studio rehearsals, clips (like the one of *Cool In The Pool*), and weird stories. Directed by Holger Czukay, broadcast on German ZDF television on April 19th, 1988.

CAN MANAGEMENT & SPOON RECORDS:
HILDEGARD SCHMIDT,
LES ROSSIGNOLS,
F - 84220 ROUSSILLON,
FRANCE.
Telefax: 33-90057004

Other music books available from *SAF*

TAPE DELAY
by Charles Neal
(ISBN 0946719 020)

256 pages of interviews, original writing, illustrations and photographs. This book is the first fully comprehensive collection to represent the ideas of the most innovative music groups of the last two decades. Contributors in alphabetical order:

Marc Almond, Dave Ball, Cabaret Voltaire, Nick Cave, Chris & Cosey, Coil, Einstürzende Neubauten, Diamanda Galas, Genesis P-Orridge, Michael Gira, The Hafler Trio, Laibach, Lydia Lunch, Matt Johnson (The The), New Order, Psychic TV, Boyd Rice (Non), Henry Rollins, Clint Ruin (Foetus), Mark E. Smith (The Fall), Sonic Youth, Stevo, Mark Stewart, Swans, Test Dept, David Tibet (Current 93).

Price £8.95 (Add £1.00 UK, £1.50 Europe, £2.00 rest of the World, for postage).

CABARET VOLTAIRE
The Art Of The Sixth Sense

by M. Fish and D. Hallbery

(ISBN 0946719 039)

This definitive second edition provides a complete critical appraisal of the group from 1973 - 1989, spanning their early dadaist dabblings in sound manipulation through to being vigorous exponents of a radical dance music.

Containing 224 pages, including over 50 photographs and a complete discography. The book is essential reading for anyone interested in music and opinions that have stretched and frayed the fringes of pop culture.

Price £6.95 (add £1.00 UK, £1.50 Europe, £2.00 rest of the World, for postage).

All titles are available mail order from SAF Publishing, PO Box 151, Harrow, Middx. HA3 0DH. UK.

All cheques/IMOs must be made payable to SAF in pounds sterling.

Credit Card orders (Access or Visa) ring 01-904 6263 (9 - 5 Weekdays)

About the Author:

Pascal Bussy is a French music journalist who has contributed articles to many music publications. He is a friend of all the members of Can, and has had a unique opportunity to interview and gain archive material from the group. On his own Tago Mago label he has released music by Can and others including; Lol Coxhill, This Heat, Vidéo-Adventures, Albert Marcoeur, Atom Crystal, Jacques Berrocal, Eyeless In Gaza, and many others. He currently lives in Paris with his wife and two children.

Thanks to:

Archie Patterson (Interview with Malcolm Mooney 1983)
Geneviève Bussy and Yuko Ishikawa (Japanese/English translation of *Doko E.*)

Photographic credits:

P. Bussy: 119, 173 (bottom left & right, middle).
EMI/Electrola: 45, 109.
Jürgen Ensthaler: 34, 42, 76, 160.
M. von Gimbut: 94.
Dietmar Kalinowsky: 88.
Werner Kirchberger: 65, 121, 122, 144 (right), 153.
Derek More: 56.
G. Reinhart: 22, 29, 37, 49, 61, 125, 129, 147, 149, 173 (top left & right).
Christian Rose: 163.
Hildegard Schmidt: 15, 16, 31, 46, 47, 51, 81, 83, 86, 87, 91, 135, 136, 139, 144 (left), 156.
United Artists: 9, 79.
Romain Urhausen: 24, 72.
Virgin Records: 5, 21, 27, 36, 39, 93 (back cover), 110, 117, 168.

Photographs not credited were unknown at the time of publication. Anyone concerned can contact the publisher and a credit will be included in future editions.

SAF Publishing, PO BOX 151, Harrow, Middx. HA3 0DH, England.